W9-BDI-987

Science Fair Projects About the Properties of Matter

Library of Congress Cataloging-in-Publication Data
Gardner, Robert, 1929–
 Science fair projects about the properties of matter, revised and expanded using the scientific method /
Robert Gardner.
     p. cm. — (Physics science projects using the scientific method)
 Summary: "Explains how to use the scientific method to conduct several science experiments about the
properties of matter. Includes ideas for science fair projects"—Provided by publisher.
 Includes bibliographical references and index.
 ISBN 978-0-7660-3417-4
 1. Matter—Properties—Experiments—Juvenile literature. 2. Science projects—Juvenile literature. I. Title.
QC173.36.G369 2010
507.8—dc22
                            2009014804
Printed in the United States of America

092009 Lake Book Manufacturing, Inc., Melrose Park, IL

10 9 8 7 6 5 4 3 2 1

Illustration Credits: Tom LaBaff and Stephanie LaBaff

Editorial Revision: Lily Book Productions

Design: Oxygen Design

Photo Credits: Shutterstock

Cover Photos: Shutterstock

Revised edition of *Science Fair Projects About the Properties of Matter Using Marbles, Water,
Balloons, and More*. Copyright © 2004.

Science Fair Projects About the Properties of Matter

Revised and Expanded
Using the Scientific Method

Robert Gardner

Enslow Publishers, Inc.
40 Industrial Road
Box 398
Berkeley Heights, NJ 07922
USA

http://www.enslow.com

Contents

Indicates activities appropriate for science fair projects.

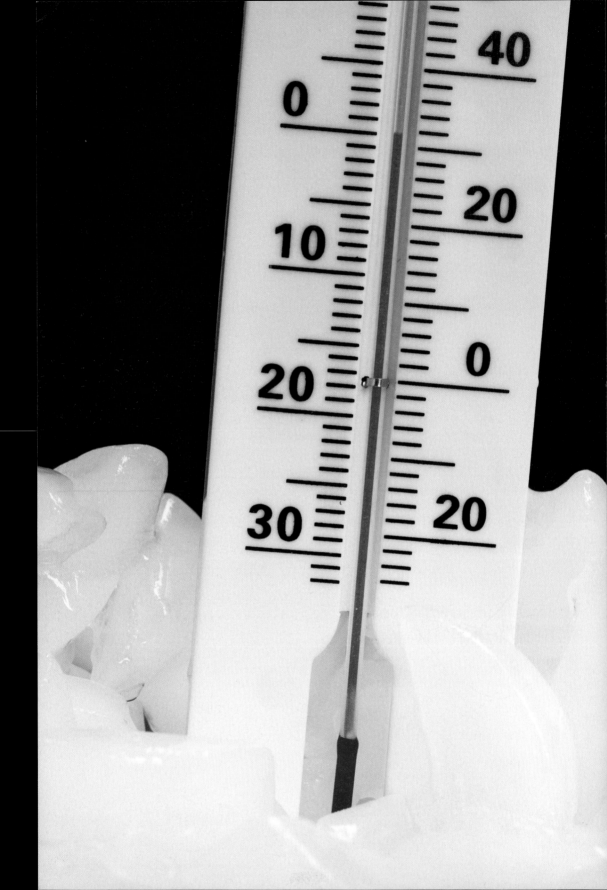

Properties of Matter Experiments and Projects Using the Scientific Method

Physics is the part of science that deals with matter and energy. You and the world around you are made up of matter. The tiniest particles of matter are atoms and molecules. These particles are much too small to be seen. More than a billion trillion molecules are present in a drop of water, which we can see. Like liquids, solids and gases are also made up of atoms and molecules.

Most gases are colorless and their molecules are far apart so they're not visible. But there's one gas, actually a combination of gases, that we often feel. That gas is air, which we become aware of when the wind blows against our faces and bodies as we run or ride our bicycles through it.

Doing the experiments in this book will allow you to unlock the secrets of matter. You'll understand why your bicycle tire sometimes goes flat, why there are gaps in railroad tracks, how thermometers work, and much more.

◄ When cooled by falling temperatures, liquid in a thermometer contracts, taking up less space and showing a lower temperature.

Experiments and Projects

This book contains lots of fun physics experiments about matter and energy. You will also be given suggestions for independent investigations that you can do yourself. Most of the experiments are followed by a section called Science Project Ideas. This section contains great ideas for your own science fair projects.

The experiments are all easy to do and safe to carry out when the instructions are followed as given. Consult with your school science teacher or some **other responsible adult** to obtain approval before starting any experiments of your own.

Most of the materials you will need to carry out the projects and experiments described in this book can be found in

How Scientists Search for Answers

When scientists have a question to answer, they start by researching. They read scientific literature and consult online science databases that are maintained by universities, research centers, or the government. There, they can study abstracts—summaries of reports—by scientists who have conducted experiments or done similar research in the field.

In this way, they find out whether other scientists have examined the same question or have tried to answer it by doing an experiment. Careful research will tell what kind of experiments, if any, have been done to try to answer the question.

Scientists do not want to repeat experiments that have known and accepted outcomes. Also, they want to avoid repeating any mistakes others may have made while doing your home. Several of the experiments may require items you can buy from a supermarket, a hobby or toy shop, a hardware store, or one of the science supply companies listed in the appendix. Some may call for articles that you may be able to borrow from your school's science department.

At times, you will need a partner to help you. It would be best if you work with friends or adults who enjoy experimenting as much as you do. That way, you will both enjoy what you are doing.

similar experiments. If no one else has done scientific work that answers the question, scientists then do further research on how best to do the experiment. While researching for the experiment, the scientist tries to guess—or predict—the possible results. This prediction is called a hypothesis.

The scientist hopes that a well-researched and carefully planned experiment will prove the hypothesis to be true. At times, however, the results of even the best-planned experiment can be far different from what the scientist expected. Yet even if the results indicate the hypothesis was not true, this does not mean the experiment was a failure. In fact, unexpected results can provide valuable information that leads to a different answer or to another, even better, experiment.

Using the Scientific Method in Experiments and Projects

The Scientific Method

A scientific experiment starts when someone wonders what would happen if certain conditions were set up and tested by following a particular process. For example, in an experiment about the effects of air pressure on matter you might ask the question: "Do different shapes create different force per area when the same amount of pressure is applied to them?" A guess about the answer is your hypothesis, and two possible hypotheses might be:

✓ Equal amounts of pressure will create equal force per area no matter what the shape of an object.

✓ The same pressure applied to objects of different shapes will result in differences in force per area.

Let's say your hypothesis is that the same pressure applied to objects of different shapes will result in differences in force per area. To test this, you push different diameter dowels into clay, using the weight (force) of the same brick.

For a start, you have to know that a scientific experiment has only two variables—that is, only two things that can change. For this experiment, one variable is the diameter of the dowels, and the other is the depth of the hole each makes in the clay.

Only the diameters of dowels you use are allowed to change—not their length, not the weight of the brick, and not how you place the brick on the dowels. If anything besides the dowel diameter were changed, it would not be possible to know what caused the depth of the hole in the clay.

Now, if your hypothesis—that the shape of an object determines force per area—turns out to be false, your experiment's results still provide important information. And those results can lead to further ideas that can be explored.

Scientists may develop logical explanations for the results of their experiments. These explanations, or theories, must be tested by more experiments. If the resulting data from experiments provide strong support for a theory, then that theory might be accepted by the world of science. But scientists are careful about accepting new theories. If any of the experiment's results contradict a theory, then that theory must be discarded, altered, or retested. That is the scientific method.

Basic Steps in the Scientific Method

The best experiments and science projects usually follow the scientific method's basic steps:

✓ Ask questions about what would happen if certain conditions or events were set up and tested in an experiment.

✓ Do background research to investigate the subject of your question.

✓ Construct a hypothesis—an answer to your question—that you can then test and investigate with an experiment.

✓ Design and conduct an experiment to test your hypothesis.

✓ Keep records, collect data, and then analyze what you have recorded.

✓ Draw a conclusion based on the experiment and the data you have recorded.

✓ Write a report about your results.

Your Hypothesis

Many experiments and science projects begin by asking whether something can be done or how it can be done. In this

book's experiment, "Pressure of Liquids, Archimedes, and Buoyancy," the question is, "How can you calculate the volume of an irregularly shaped object?"

To come up with a hypothesis, you first study ways that the volume of an object is calculated. You will learn about Archimedes, the philosopher of ancient Greece whose hypothesis was: "The volume is calculated by measuring how much water the object displaces when submerged."

You also need to find out how to design an experiment to test your hypothesis. What methods and equipment are needed to test your hypothesis? By using the right tools and materials you can study and record the results of your experiments.

Remember: To give your experiment or project every chance of success, prepare a hypothesis that is clear and brief. The simpler the hypothesis the better it is.

Designing the Experiment

Your experiment will investigate whether the hypothesis is true or false. The experiment is intended to test the hypothesis, not necessarily to prove that the hypothesis is right.

The results of a well-designed experiment are more valuable than the results of an experiment that is intentionally designed to give the answer you want. The conditions you set up in your experiment must be a fair test of your hypothesis. For example, in an experiment measuring how much water is displaced by irregularly shaped objects, you have to carefully measure the displaced water. That means you will need a good measuring cup and will use the same cup for each measurement.

By carefully carrying out your experiment, you will discover useful information that can be recorded as data (observations).

It is most important that the experiment's procedures and results are as accurate as possible. Design the experiment for observable, measurable results. And keep it simple, because the more complicated your experiment is, the more chance you have for error.

Also, if you have friends helping you with an experiment or project, make sure from the start that they will take their tasks seriously.

Remember: Scientists around the world always use metric measurements in their experiments and projects, and so should you. Use metric liquid and dry measures and a Celsius thermometer.

Recording Data

Your hypothesis, procedure, data, and conclusions should be recorded immediately as you experiment, but do not keep it on loose scraps of paper. Record your data in a notebook or logbook—one you use just for experiments. Your notebook should be bound so that you have a permanent record. The laboratory notebook is an essential part of all academic and scientific research.

Make sure to include the date, experiment number, and a brief description of how you collected the data. Write clearly. If you have to cross something out, do it with just a single line, then rewrite the correct information.

Repeat your experiment several times to be sure your results are consistent and your data are trustworthy. Do not try to interpret data as you go along. It is better first to record results accurately, then study them later.

You might even find that you want to replace your experiment's original question with a new one. For example, the question, "Do solid objects sink because they are more dense than water?" could bring up another question: "If so, then how can steel ships float?"

Writing the Science Fair Report

Communicate the results of your experiment by writing a clear report. Even the most successful experiment loses its value if the scientist can not clearly tell what happened. Your report should describe how the experiment was designed and conducted and should state its precise results.

Following are the parts of a science fair report, in the order they should appear:

• **Title Page**

The title of your experiment should be centered and near the top of the page. Your teacher will tell you what other information is needed, such as your name, grade, and the name of your science teacher.

• **Table of Contents**

On the report's second page, list the remaining parts of the report and their page numbers.

• **Abstract**

Give a brief overview of your experiment. In just a few sentences, tell the purpose of the experiment, what you did, and what you found out. Always write in plain, clear language.

• Introduction

State your hypothesis and explain how you came up with it. Discuss your experiment's main question and how your research led to the hypothesis. Tell what you hoped to achieve when you started the experiment.

• Experiment and Data

This is a detailed step-by-step explanation of how you organized and carried out the experiment. Explain what methods you followed and what materials and equipment you used.

State when the experiment was done (the date and perhaps the time of day) and under what conditions (in a laboratory, outside on a windy day, in cold or warm weather, etc.). Tell who was involved and what part they played in the experiment. Include clearly labeled graphs and tables of data from the experiment as well as any photographs or drawings that help illustrate your work. Anyone who reads your report should be able to repeat the experiment just the way you did it. (Repeating an experiment is a good way to test whether the original results were obtained correctly.)

• Discussion

Explain your results and conclusions, perhaps comparing them with published scientific data you first read about in your research. Consider how the experiment's results relate to your hypothesis. Ask yourself: Do my results support or contradict my hypothesis? Then analyze the answer.

Would you do anything differently if you did this experiment again? State what you have learned as a result of the experiment.

Analyze how your tools and equipment did their tasks, and how well you and others used those tools. If you think the experiment could be done better if designed another way or if you have another hypothesis that might be tested, then include this in your discussion.

• Conclusion

Make a brief summary of you experiment's results. Include only information and data already stated in the report, and be sure not to bring in any new information.

• Acknowledgments

Give credit to everyone who helped you with the experiment. State the names of these individuals and briefly explain who they are and how they assisted you.

• References / Bibliography

List any books, magazines, journals, articles, Web sites, scientific databases, and interviews that were important to your research for the experiment.

Science Fairs

Science fair judges tend to reward creative thought and imagination. It is difficult to be creative or imaginative unless you are really interested in your project. So, be sure to choose a subject that appeals to you. And before you jump into a project, consider your own talents and the cost of materials you will need.

Remember, judges at science fairs do not reward projects or experiments that are simply copied from a book or show little thought. A diagram or model of an atom or molecule would not impress most judges; however, a unique method

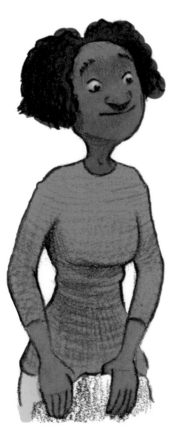

for measuring the size of molecules would gain serious consideration.

If you decide to use a project from this book for a science fair, you should find ways to modify or extend it. This should not be difficult because, as you do these projects, ideas for new experiments probably will come to mind. These experiments could make excellent science fair projects, particularly because the ideas are your own and are interesting to you.

If you decide to enter a science fair and have never done so before, you should read some of the books listed in the Further Reading section and visit the Internet sites. The books and sites that refer to science fairs provide plenty of hints and information to help avoid the pitfalls that sometimes plague first-time entrants. You will learn how to prepare appealing reports that include charts and graphs, how to set up and display your work, how to present your project, and how to relate to judges and visitors.

Following are some suggestions to consider.

Some Tips for Success at a Science Fair

Science teachers and science fair judges have many different opinions on what makes a good science fair project or experiment. Here are the most important elements:

Originality of Concept is one of the most important things judges consider. Some judges believe that the best science fair projects answer a question that is not found in a science textbook.

Scientific Content is another main area of evaluation. How was science applied in the procedure? Are there sufficient data? Did you stick to your intended procedure and keep good records?

Thoroughness is next in importance. Was the experiment repeated as often as needed to test your hypothesis? Is your notebook complete, and are the data accurate? Does your research bibliography show you did enough library work?

Clarity in how you present your exhibit shows you had a good understanding of the subject you worked on. It is important that your exhibit clearly presents the results of your work.

Effective Process: Judges recognize that how skillfully you carry out a science fair project is usually more important than its results. A well-done project gives students the best understanding of what scientists actually do day-to-day.

Remember: Do not block your exhibit. Stand to the side when someone is looking at it.

Other points to consider when preparing for your science fair:

The Abstract: Write up a brief explanation of your project and make copies for visitors or judges who want to read it.

Knowledge: Be ready to answer questions from visitors and judges confidently. Know what is in your notebook and make some notes on index cards to remind you of important points.

Practice: Before the science fair begins, prepare a list of several questions you think you might be asked. Think about the answers and about how your display can help to support them. Have a friend or parent ask you questions and answer them out loud. Knowing your work thoroughly helps you feel more confident when you are asked about it.

Appearance: Dress and act in a way that shows you take your project seriously. Visitors and judges should get the impression that you are interested in the project and take pride in answering their questions about it.

Physics projects about the properties of matter can be photographed or sketched. Many projects are colorful, so use color to make pictures more striking. Photograph or draw any special laboratory tools or apparatus you set up. Be inventive about different ways of showing what took place.

Safety First

It is your responsibility to use all materials and equipment only as directed in this book. The precautions necessary to prevent accidents and to make the experiments safe and enjoyable are easy to follow.

✔ It is essential that **all investigations and science fair projects be approved by a responsible adult.** Where warranted, the experimentation should take place **under adult supervision.** If there are any questions about safety, **the adult** should be sure to obtain the approval of a science teacher before allowing the experiments.

✔ Wear approved goggles (**safety glasses**) when you are working with a flame or doing anything that might cause injury to your eyes. Goggles can be purchased in hardware or dollar stores.

✔ Read all instructions carefully before proceeding with a project. If you have questions, check with your supervisor before going any further.

✔ Never use a mercury thermometer because exposure to mercury is dangerous; use mercury-free alternatives, such as thermometers containing alcohol.

✔ Maintain a serious attitude while conducting experiments. Fooling around can be dangerous to you and to others.

✔ Never let water droplets come in contact with a hot lightbulb.

✔ Never experiment with household electricity except under the supervision of a knowledgeable **adult**.

✔ It is a good idea to wear an apron and to work on surfaces that can resist water damage. Covering a surface with newspapers or plastic sheeting will help to protect it.

And now, on to the experiments!

CHAPTER 1

CHAPTER 1

Atoms, Molecules, and Matter

Matter appears to us as solids, liquids, and gases. These are called the three states of matter. (Plasma is the fourth state of matter found in and between stars, but we will not consider it in this book.) But matter is actually made up of tiny particles much too small for us to see. Although scientists have identified thousands of different substances, they are all made up of only about one hundred different kinds of atoms. Substances that have only one kind of atom are called elements. You are probably familiar with some of them. They include such substances as copper, aluminum, iron, carbon, helium, hydrogen, and oxygen.

Atoms are very small. A cubic centimeter of aluminum, for example, contains 2.2 zetta atoms.

◄ The Atomium in Brussels, Belgium, rises 102 meters. Nine steel balls are connected to model the atomic structure of an iron crystal.

A zetta is a very big number; it is 1,000,000,000,000,000,000,000. Think about trying to divide a cubic centimeter into 2.2 zetta parts. You will then understand why we can not see atoms.

A molecule is defined as the smallest part of a substance that can exist as that substance. Some elements, such as helium and neon, exist as huge numbers of atoms. In such cases, the atom is also a molecule of the element and can be represented by the element's symbol. For example, He represents one atom of helium.

The molecules of other elements contain more than one atom. For example, molecules of the elements oxygen and hydrogen contain two atoms of the element. These molecules can be represented by symbols, O_2 for oxygen and H_2 for hydrogen. A periodic table of the elements, found in many science classrooms, shows all the elements and the symbols for each of them.

The molecules that make up most substances contain atoms of more than one element. Such substances are termed compounds. Water is a compound. Its molecules contain two atoms of hydrogen and one atom of oxygen. Therefore, the molecular formula for water is H_2O. In the previous paragraph, H_2 means two atoms of hydrogen in a hydrogen molecule. In water molecules (H_2O), there are two atoms of hydrogen (H) and one of oxygen (O). The symbol H_2 can mean two atoms in the element's molecule. When written as H_2O, it means two atoms of hydrogen combined with one atom of oxygen in a molecule of the compound water.

A theory of matter was first proposed about two hundred years ago by the English chemist John Dalton. The four points of Dalton's theory make a good summary of our first discussion of matter:

✔ All elements are made of indestructible particles called atoms.

✔ Atoms of the same element are identical to each other but different from those of any other element.

✔ Atoms can join together (bond) to form molecules, the basic particles of compounds.

✔ Chemical reactions occur when atoms change their bonding arrangements to form new substances.

The first part of Dalton's theory explains why matter, itself, can not be destroyed or created: Atoms are indestructible. The second part of his theory explains why elements can not be changed into anything simpler: Atoms are the fundamental particles of matter. The third part of the theory explains why there are so many compounds: The one hundred or so types of atoms can combine in many, many ways. The combining of compounds or the decomposing (breaking apart) of compounds are explained by the fourth part of Dalton's theory.

EXPERIMENT 1.1

Molecules and the States of Matter

Question:

Do the three states of matter all have a definite shape and volume?

Hypothesis:

No. Only solids have definite shapes and volumes.

Materials:

- metric measuring cup
- 100-mL graduated cylinder
- balloon
- rigid plastic syringe
- water

For the most part, matter exists in three states, solid, liquid, or gas. A solid has a definite shape and volume. You can confirm this definition by looking at any solid substance—a table made of wood, for instance.

A liquid has a definite volume, but its shape can vary. To confirm this, pour 100 milliliters (mL) of water from a metric measuring cup into a 100-mL graduated cylinder. Has the liquid's volume changed? Has its shape changed?

A gas has neither a definite shape nor a definite volume. To see that this is true, blow up a balloon with the gas (air) from your lungs. The air that fills the balloon takes the shape and volume of the filled balloon. Before you blew up the balloon, the air had the shape and volume of the insides of your lungs. Let the air out of the balloon. The gas mixes with the air in the room, which has the shape and volume of the room.

Here is another way to see the difference between a gas and a liquid.

Procedure:

1. Fill a rigid plastic syringe with air by pulling back the piston as shown in Figure 1a.

2. Then hold your finger firmly over the open end and try to push the piston inward (Figure 1b). Can you squeeze the gas into a smaller volume?

3. Now, fill the syringe with water as shown in Figure 1c. Can you squeeze the water into a smaller volume?

4. Can you squeeze a solid such as a rock or a steel rod into a smaller volume?

Figure 1.

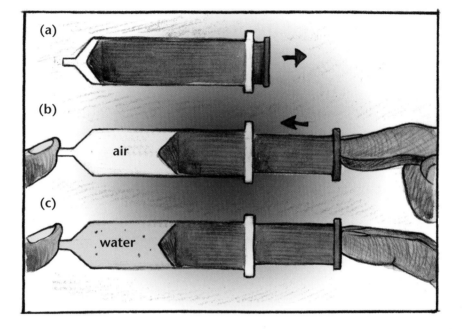

a) Partially fill a syringe with air.
b) Put your finger firmly over the end of the syringe and try to push
   the piston inward. Can you squeeze the gas into a smaller volume?
c) Partially fill the syringe with water. Can you squeeze water into a
   smaller volume?

Results and Conclusions

Water (a liquid) and rock or steel (solids) cannot be squeezed into smaller

volumes. Air (a gas), however, can be compressed into a smaller volume.

EXPERIMENT 1.2

A Model for the Three States of Matter

Question:
Can you build a model to show the three states of matter?

Hypothesis:
You can use a box and marbles to demonstrate how the states of matter are affected by the distance between molecules.

Materials:
- 50 or more marbles
- box or tray with steep sides

You can build a simple model to show the three states of matter. You will need a box or a tray with steep sides.

Figure 2.

Marbles in a box can be used to represent atoms or molecules in any of the three states of matter.

Procedure:

1. Put 50 or more marbles in the tray. Tip the tray up at an angle so that the marbles all collect at one end, as shown in Figure 2.

Notice how they line up touching one another in straight rows. This arrangement of marbles represents atoms (or molecules) in *solid* matter. The bottom and sides of the box provide the force that holds the "atoms" together. In a real solid, the atoms are held together by attractive electrical forces called chemical bonds.

2. Keeping the tray tilted, jiggle it gently but rapidly in your hands. See how the "atoms" or "molecules" vibrate while staying in place.

   This represents a solid at, let's say, room temperature. The speed at which molecules move increases with temperature. Consequently, at a higher temperature, the particles would vibrate faster. At still higher temperatures, the increased vibrations allow the atoms to *momentarily* break away from their neighbors and form bonds with new atoms. The movement results in less order, more open spaces, and the ability of the atoms to flow. This condition is a model of a substance *melting*, which results in a liquid.

3. Now, decrease the tilt of the tray and gradually increase the jiggling until the marbles no longer stay in their ordered rows. Even though they still touch each other, they now change positions, slide over one another and move farther.

4. Turn the tray slightly to one side. Notice that the "atoms" now "flow" as a group. The marbles now represent the molecules in *liquid* matter. The atoms or molecules in a liquid are not as ordered or as tightly packed as in a solid.

5. Next, put the tray on a flat surface and shake it vigorously. Notice how the marbles fill the entire tray, bouncing off each other and off the tray's walls in a chaotic manner. The marbles now separate from one another. They move in straight lines until they collide with other marbles or the walls of the tray. The model now represents a *gas*.

Results and Conclusions

At high temperatures, which can be compared to you vigorously shaking the marbles, the molecules have enough energy to overcome the attractive forces that held them together. The separation of the marbles and their straight line paths from collision to collision represents the change from liquid to gas, or vaporization.

Your model has only one layer of atoms. Real matter would consist of many layers of atoms or molecules.

Some substances melt and vaporize at higher temperatures than others. The differences in melting and boiling temperatures are due to differences in the attractive forces that hold atoms or molecules together in the solid and liquid state. The stronger the bonds, the greater the temperature needed to break them. And higher temperature in the molecular world means stronger vibrations. The molecules in liquid hydrogen must be held together by very weak forces because hydrogen melts at −262°C (−440°F) and boils at −253°C (−422°F). On the other hand, the attractive forces between atoms of tungsten metal must be very strong. It boils at 5,930°C (10,706°F) and melts at 3,680°C (6,656°F).

When a substance melts or boils, the energy that is added by heating causes the molecules of the substance to move faster and overcome the attractive forces between them. This energy does not increase the speed of the atoms. Consequently, the temperature remains constant when substances melt or boil.

EXPERIMENT 1.3

Brownian Motion:
Evidence for Atoms

Question:

How can you see the effects of air on molecules?

Hypothesis:

You cannot see atoms or molecules, but you can see the effects of the fluid or air around them using a microscope.

Materials:

- **an adult**
- Brownian motion apparatus
- candle
- matches
- microscope
- flashlight

In 1827, Robert Brown, a Scottish botanist, was using his microscope to examine some pollen suspended in water. He noticed that the pollen grains seemed to bounce about rather than remaining still. It was a generation later before anyone could explain this phenomenon, which came to be known as Brownian motion.

Ask to borrow a Brownian motion apparatus (Figure 3) from your school's science department. You will also need to borrow a microscope if you do not have one.

Procedure:

1. **Have an adult** light a candle. Once the candle is burning well, **ask the adult** to blow it out.

2. Immediately squeeze the rubber bulb located on one side of the Brownian motion apparatus and hold the inlet tube in the smoke. Then release the bulb so that smoke will be drawn into the viewing chamber.

3. Clamp the base of the apparatus to a microscope stage.

4. Shine a flashlight onto the lens of the apparatus to illuminate the smoke particles.

Figure 3.

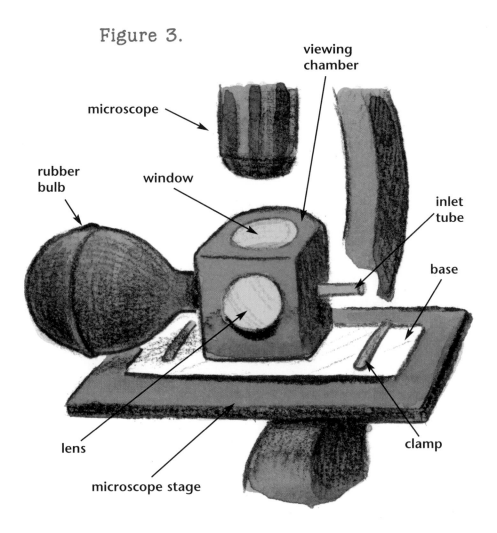

With a Brownian motion apparatus and a microscope, you can see the effects of fast-moving air molecules on smoke particles.

Results and Conclusions

When viewed through the window of the apparatus under the microscope's low power (50X or 100X), the smoke particles will appear as bright points of light. Notice how they bounce about as they are struck by fast-moving molecules of air.

The effect of liquid or air on microscopic particles is described by Brownian motion. When molecules of air or liquid bounce into the microscopic particles, such as pollen or smoke, the particles move.

 Science Project Idea

- Obtain some pollen and see if you can make the same observation that Brown made. What else can you use in order to observe Brownian motion?

EXPERIMENT 1.4

How Big Are Molecules?

Question:

How can you estimate the size of molecules?

Hypothesis:

You can estimate their size by reducing them
to very thin layers.

Materials:

- water
- large flat tray, such as
  a cafeteria tray
- chalk dust from
  blackboard eraser
- piece of fine wire
- clothespin
- rubbing alcohol

- oleic acid
  (obtain from school
  science department
  or science supply
  company)
- a partner
- magnifier
- metric ruler

Molecules are very small, but you can estimate their size. You have
probably seen the rainbow-colored film that forms when a thin layer of
motor oil floats on a puddle of water. Substances insoluble in water and
less dense than water will float and spread out into a very thin layer when
added to water. One such substance is oleic acid. It spreads out until it is
one or two molecules thick. By finding the thickness of the oleic acid, you
can estimate the size of oleic acid molecules.

Procedure:

1. Pour water onto a very clean, large, flat tray, such as the kind found in cafeterias. The water should be about a centimeter (about ½ inch) deep.

2. When the water is still, sprinkle some powdery chalk dust on its surface. This can be done by tapping a well-used blackboard eraser above the water.

3. Next, bend a fine piece of wire into a narrow V-shape as shown in Figure 4a. Wind the ends of the wire together and clamp them with a clothespin.

4. Dip the V-shaped part of the wire into some rubbing alcohol to clean it. When the wire dries, dip the very tip of the V into oleic acid. Only a tiny drop should cling to the wire.

5. To estimate the drop's volume, ask a partner to hold the clothespin while you use a magnifier and a ruler to estimate the diameter of the drop as shown in Figure 4b. To make the calculation easy, assume the drop is a cube. Then simply multiply the diameter by itself twice (d x d x d). What do you estimate the drop's volume to be?

6. Dip the tip of the wire into the center of the water in the tray. The drop of oleic acid will spread out and push the fine powder outward forming a circle. The circle is a thin layer of oleic acid. Dip the wire tip into the water several times to be sure all the oleic acid is on the water.

7. Measure the average diameter of the circular layer of oleic acid. Then calculate the area covered by the oleic acid remembering that the area of a circle is πr^2. You probably know that π (pi) is approximately 3.14. The thickness (t) of the oleic acid times its area is equal to its volume:

$$\pi r^2 \times t = volume$$

To find the thickness, divide the volume by the area:

$$t = volume \div \pi r^2$$

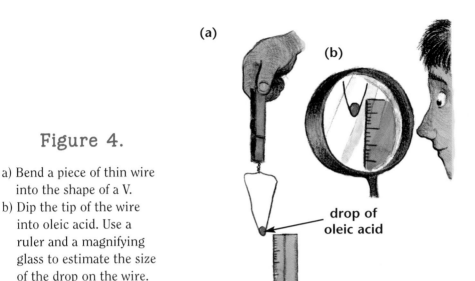

Figure 4.

a) Bend a piece of thin wire into the shape of a V.
b) Dip the tip of the wire into oleic acid. Use a ruler and a magnifying glass to estimate the size of the drop on the wire.

(a)

(b)

drop of oleic acid

Results and Conclusions

You will find that the thickness is very small. For example, suppose the diameter of the drop is 0.5 mm and the diameter of the circle of oleic acid on the water is 20 cm. The volume of the drop is approximately:

0.5 mm x 0.5 mm x 0.5 mm = 0.125 cubic millimeters (mm^3)

The area covered by the oleic acid is:

πr^2 = 3.14 x 10 cm x 10 cm = 314 cm^2

Then the thickness of the layer of oleic acid is:

t = volume ÷ area = 0.125 mm^3 ÷ 314 cm^2

You can not divide mm^3 by cm^2, so you need to change square centimeters to square millimeters. Since 1 cm = 10 mm, one square centimeter equals 10 mm x 10 mm = 100 mm^2.

Now you can calculate the thickness of the oleic acid.

t = 0.125 mm^3 ÷ 31400 mm^2 = 0.00000398 mm

Using your measurements, what do you estimate is the size of a molecule of oleic acid?

EXPERIMENT 1.5

Conservation of Matter

Question:

Can matter be created or destroyed?

Hypothesis:

No, and you can show this by carrying out experiments that change matter's form and then weighing the substances that result.

Materials:

- **an adult**
- balance
- paper
- salt
- plastic vials with tight-fitting caps
- water
- notebook
- pen or pencil
- ice
- paper towel
- lead nitrate crystals
- Epsom salt (magnesium sulfate)

According to Dalton's atomic theory of matter, atoms are indestructible and molecules are made up of atoms. According to the theory, matter can not be created or destroyed because atoms are indestructible. To test this idea, you can carry out some experiments in which you change matter in various ways. You can then check to see if you still have the same amount (weight) of matter you started with.

We choose to measure matter in terms of weight because measuring matter by volume is often unsatisfactory. For example, as you saw in Experiment 1.1, you can easily change the volume of a gas by squeezing it. If you dissolve salt or alcohol in water, the total volume actually shrinks. Furthermore, grainy solids such as salt and sand contain air spaces between the particles. The volume of that air must be measured before we can determine the actual volume of a grainy solid.

Does Weight Change
When a Solid Dissolves in a Liquid?

Procedure:

1. On a balance, place a piece of paper and add 2 g of salt.

2. Next, add to the balance pan a vial that is about three-fourths filled with water along with a cap that fits the vial. Record the total weight of vial, water, cap, paper, and salt.

3. Carefully pour the salt into the water. Place the cap securely on the vial and wait for the salt to dissolve.

4. After the salt has dissolved, reweigh the vial with the solution and its cap together with the piece of paper. Has dissolving brought about any change in weight?

Does Weight Change When Ice Melts?

Procedure:

1. Place a piece of ice in another vial. Snap the cover on the vial and weigh the vial and its contents. If any moisture condenses on the outside of the vial, be sure to wipe it off with a paper towel before you weigh the vial.

2. Record the weight of the vial and ice.

3. After the ice has melted, reweigh the vial and the melted ice (water). (Again, if moisture has condensed on the vial, wipe it dry before weighing.) Did melting bring about any change in weight?

Does Weight Change During a Chemical Reaction?

Procedure:

1. **Ask an adult** to prepare a solution of lead nitrate by adding 1.5 g of lead nitrate crystals to 10 mL of distilled water in a vial.

2. Meanwhile, you can prepare a solution of Epsom salt (magnesium sulfate) by adding 1.2 g of Epsom salt to 10 mL of water in another vial.

3. Place the two vials and their contents on a balance pan and record the total weight of the vials and the solutions they contain.

4. Carefully pour the solution in one vial into the solution in the other vial. Weigh the vial with the solution and the empty vial.

Results and Conclusions

You will see that a new substance is formed. Because a new substance has formed, you have witnessed a chemical reaction. Did the chemical reaction bring about a change in weight?

Discard the solution and white solid into a sink and rinse with lots of water.

Science Project Ideas

- Design and carry out an experiment to show that the total volume actually decreases when salt or alcohol dissolves in water.

- What is the chemical reaction that occurs when a solution of Epsom salt is added to a solution of lead nitrate?

About Weight and Mass

Many people confuse mass and weight. In the last experiment, you probably measured weight in grams. To be more correct, you were measuring mass. Mass, the amount of matter in an object, is measured on a balance. An easy way to understand the difference between mass and weight is to think about taking a trip to the moon. Suppose that on Earth your mass, as determined on a large balance, is 50 kilograms (kg). Your weight, which can be determined by suspending you from a spring scale, would be 490 N (newtons). Your weight, therefore, is the force with which the earth pulls you toward its center. It is the force we refer to as gravity. (A newton is the force needed to move one kilogram with an acceleration of one meter per second per second.)

When you reach the moon, you will find that your mass, as determined on an equal-arm balance, is still 50 kg. There is no more or less of you. When suspended from a spring balance, your weight, however, will be only 67 N. The reason is that the force of gravity on the moon is about one-sixth as large as it is on Earth. In other words, mass is the amount of matter in an object, while weight is the force gravity exerts on it.

A balance is used to measure mass. An unknown mass is placed on one pan (usually the one on your left). Known masses are placed on the other pan until the balance beam is level. The level beam shows that the masses are equal. Because gravity pulls with the same force on equal masses, the effects of gravity cancel out. Consequently, a kilogram of mass will be balanced by a standard kilogram on the moon just as it will on Earth.

The kilogram is the standard unit for measuring mass. The most common smaller unit is the gram (g), which is $\frac{1}{1,000}$ of a kilogram, but milligrams ($\frac{1}{1,000}$ of a gram) are also commonly used. You may have seen labels on pill bottles that give the mass of each pill in milligrams (mg). The U.S. customary system of measurement uses pounds, ounces, and a variety of other units.

On Earth, objects weigh about 0.5 percent more at the poles than at the equator. This is because Earth's gravitational pull is slightly stronger at the poles than at the equator. In this book we will not make a big distinction between mass and weight because within half a percent the mass and weight of objects on Earth are proportional. In this book we will use the familiar unit, gram, to measure both mass and weight. However, for the sake of correctness, we will use the unit grams-weight rather than grams to speak of an object's weight.

CHAPTER 2

Elastic Properties of Solids and Liquids

As you found in the previous chapter, all matter consists of atoms and molecules. These tiny particles that make up solids and liquids must attract one another because the matter holds together. The attractive force between atoms or molecules of the same element or compound is called *cohesion*. The attractive force between atoms or molecules of different substances is called *adhesion*.

The cohesive force between two molecules or atoms is very small. However, the combined attraction of billions of molecules within a small bit of matter is huge. For example, a steel cable 2.5 cm (1 in) in diameter can be used to lift more than 23,000 kg (50,000 lb or 25 tons).

Solids, such as wood, concrete, and steel, are used to build houses, skyscrapers, bridges, cars, and many other things. These structures are subject to stresses that tend to

◀ San Francisco's Golden Gate Bridge is a suspension bridge, built to withstand the tension caused by the constant stretching of the supporting cables.

separate the atoms or molecules of which they are made. When you walk across a floor, there is a stress on it. Your weight tends to bend the floor. The many cars and trucks on a bridge tend to bend the bridge.

Figure 5.
Examples of Stress

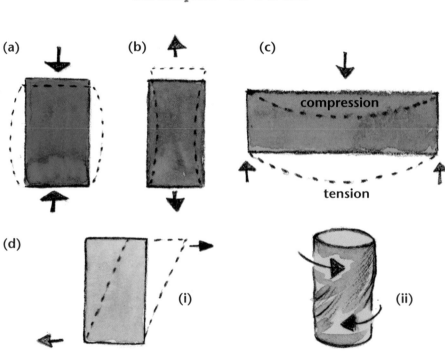

The arrows show the direction of the forces that create the stress.
a) compression;
b) tension;
c) bending;
d) (i) shear; (ii) torsional (twisting) shear.

Solids are able to withstand stresses because they are elastic. They can be stretched, compressed, and bent because their molecules can be separated or pushed together by small amounts. The basic types of stress are compression, tension, bending, and shearing (see Figure 5).

✔ Compression is caused by forces that push inward on a structure. A vertical support column is an example of a structure being compressed.

✔ Tension occurs when forces tend to stretch a structure. The springs or cables that support a suspension bridge are examples of stress due to tension. Forces of tension can be found on the surface of liquids, as you will learn later. Such forces result in what is called *surface tension.*

✔ Bending is a combination of tension and compression. A beam supporting a load will bend. The top of the beam undergoes compression, while the bottom is stretched and so experiences tension.

✔ Shearing arises when one part of a structure is pushed sideways relative to another part. A rivet holding two pieces of metal together experiences shear stress if the pieces of metal are pulled in opposite directions. Torsional shear occurs when twisting forces are applied. For example, you apply torsional shear when you open a bottle that has a twist-off cap.

EXPERIMENT 2.1

Investigating Compression and Tension

Question:

Can you measure compression and tension strength of everyday materials?

Hypothesis:

Yes, you can easily measure the compression and tensile strength of paper.

Materials:

- 8½-x-11-inch sheets of paper
- spring-type bathroom scale
- book
- paper and plastic soda straws
- tape
- scissors
- plastic pail
- rubber tubing or other soft padding
- wooden dowel
- sink
- a friend
- pencil or pen

Buildings, bridges, and towers rest on foundations that are usually made of concrete and steel. These foundations must be able to withstand compression. The decks of suspension bridges hang from cables. The cables are subjected to huge tension forces. Use paper to see how such compression and tension forces work.

Figure 6.

Testing the Compression
Strength of Paper

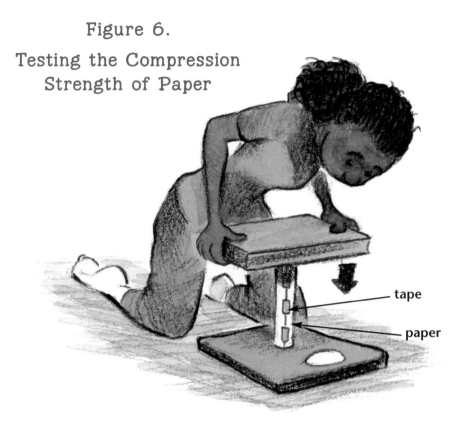

tape

paper

Roll a sheet of paper into a cylinder and tape it together. Place the paper cylinder on a bathroom scale. Put a book on the cylinder and push down. What is the compression strength of the paper?

Procedure:

1. Roll a sheet of 8½-x-11-in paper into a hollow cylinder and tape it together as shown in Figure 6.

2. Place the paper cylinder on a bathroom scale and push straight down on the tube with a book. How much force is needed before the book falls as the tube crushes?

3. Is the compression strength of the tube affected by its shape? To find out, you can crease paper cylinders to make tubes that are square, rectangular, or triangular in cross section.

Results and Conclusions

What do you find? What is the compression strength of a paper soda straw? Look closely at the straw. Is it rolled in the same way as the paper cylinder you made? If not, why do you think it is rolled differently? How do the compression strengths of paper and plastic soda straws compare?

Procedure:

1. To test the strength of paper under tension, wrap rubber tubing or some soft padding around the handle of a plastic pail. Tape a paper loop around the handle of the pail as shown in Figure 7a. Slip a wooden dowel through the paper loop so you can lift the pail with your hands as shown.

2. Hold the pail over a sink or take it outside. Have a friend add water to the pail being careful not to wet the paper.

3. After the pail's weight breaks the paper, you can weigh the pail and water on a bathroom scale.

Results and Conclusions

What force (weight) was needed to overcome the paper's tensile strength? Does the length of the paper loop affect its tensile strength? Carry out an experiment to find out.

Procedure:

1. Does shape affect tensile strength? To find out, cut a sheet of 8½-x-11-in paper into strips that are about 8½ inches long and about ¾-inch wide. Some of the shapes you might try are shown in Figure 7b. You can also design some shapes of your own.

(a)

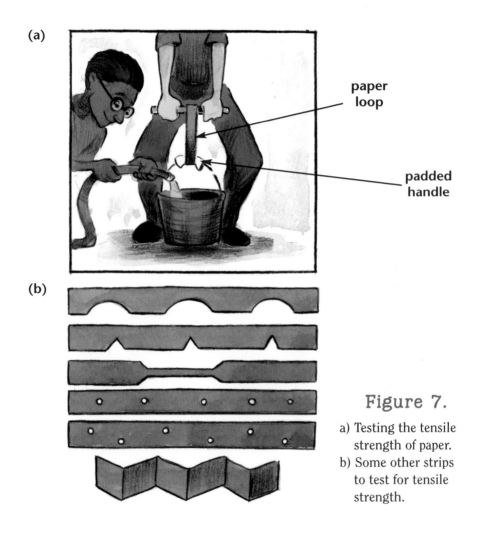

paper
loop

padded
handle

(b)

Figure 7.

a) Testing the tensile
   strength of paper.
b) Some other strips
   to test for tensile
   strength.

2. Mark a point on each strip where you think it will break.

3. Pull on the ends of the strips until they break. If you can not break
   them, get someone to pull on one end while you pull on the other.

Results and Conclusions

Did the strips break where you thought they would? Why do you think
each strip broke where it did?

Science Project Ideas

- Test some other paper tubes to find their compression strength. Does the diameter of the tube affect its compression strength? Does the thickness of the tube affect its compression strength? Does doubling the thickness double the compression strength? Are some types of paper stronger than others?

- Test the tensile strength of different brands of paper towels being sure to keep the width and length of the loops all the same. Which brand is the strongest? The weakest?

- Measure the tensile strength of different kinds of paper such as wrapping, writing, newspaper, facial, etc. Which kind is the strongest? The weakest?

- Design and carry out experiments to test the compression and tensile strength of materials other than paper.

- Early experiments on the elasticity of a solid under tension were performed by Robert Hooke, a seventeenth-century English scientist. His experiments led to what has come to be known as Hooke's Law. See if you can duplicate Hooke's experiments and confirm his law.

EXPERIMENT 2.2

Investigating Bending Stress

Question:
How is bending affected by the length of a beam?

Hypothesis:
The longer the beam, the more it can sag. This is especially true when weight is suspended from the center.

Materials:
- 2 metersticks or yardsticks
- 2 tables of equal height
- string
- plastic pail
- water
- measuring cup
- ruler
- a friend
- paper and plastic soda straws

The beams found in buildings and bridges are there to support the weight placed on them. The bending they undergo produces compression and tension as you saw in Figure 5c.

Procedure:

1. To see how bending is affected by the length of a beam, place a meterstick or yardstick between two tables as shown in Figure 8a. The edges of the tables should be 60 cm (24 in) apart. The 15-cm (6-in) and 76-cm (30-in) markings on the meterstick (or yardstick) should be even with the edges of the tables.

2. Use a string to hang a plastic pail from the middle of the stick.

3. Lay another meterstick or yardstick beside the first one. It will be used as a reference for measuring how much the middle of the other stick bends when a load is suspended from it.

4. Pour water into the pail ½ a cup at a time. Do this until the middle of the stick, as indicated by a ruler, is 2.5 cm (1 in) lower than the other stick. How much water did you add? How much does it weigh? (One cup of water weighs approximately 0.20 kg [7 oz]).

5. Next, move the tables closer together until the span between them is 30 cm (12 in). Then the 30-cm (12-in) and 60-cm (24-in) marks on the stick should be even with the edges of the tables. How much does the stick bend now under the same stress? Does halving the length of the beam halve the bending?

Results and Conclusions

Shape and orientation play an important role in placing beams. For example, what do you think will happen to the bending strength of the meterstick (or yardstick) if you turn it on its edge as shown in Figure 8a?

Figure 8.

(a)

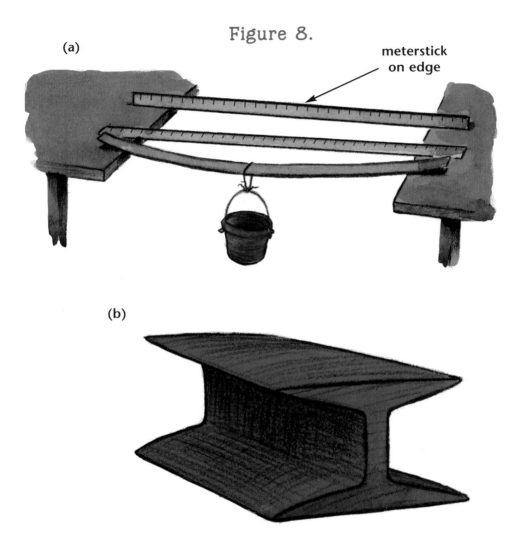

meterstick
on edge

(b)

a) The drawing shows an experiment set up to measure the effect of bending
   stress on a flat meterstick. Does the resistance to bending stress change
   when the meterstick is turned onto its narrow edge?
b) Why are I-shaped steel beams used in construction?

Procedure:

1. Move the tables so that the span is again 60 cm (2 ft). Turn the meterstick or yardstick on its narrow edge. Have a friend support the stick near each end. Then hang the same weight as before from the middle of the meterstick (or yardstick).

Results and Conclusions

How much does the stick bend now? How has the orientation of the beam affected its bending strength?

Devise a way to compare the bending strength of paper and plastic soda straws. How do the compression and bending strengths of these straws compare?

 Science Project Ideas

- Design and conduct experiments to find out how thickness and width affect the bending of a beam.

- Design and conduct experiments to find out how bending is affected by the kind of material used to span the gap.

- Why do you think I-shaped steel beams are used in heavy construction? (The top and bottom of an I beam are wide, but the middle part of the beam is narrow. See Figure 8b.)

EXPERIMENT 2.3

Squares, Triangles, and Shear Stresses

Question:

Which resist shear stresses better, rectangles or triangles?

Hypothesis:

Triangles are stronger than rectangles.

Materials:

- plastic soda straws
- common pins
- masking tape

Procedure:

1. Use plastic soda straws and common pins to build the square or rectangular structure shown in Figure 9a. **Cover the sharp ends of the pins with masking tape**.

Figure 9.

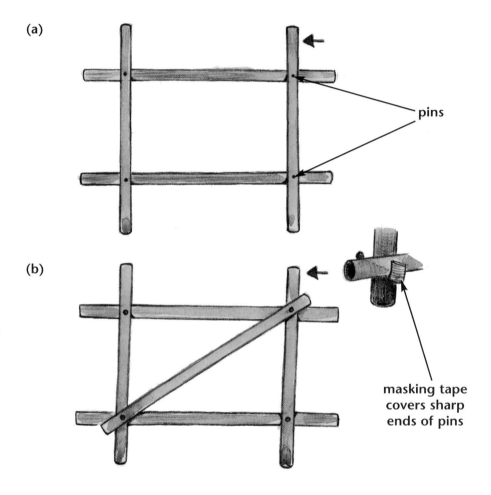

a) Apply a shear force, as shown by the arrow, to a rectangular structure.
b) How does the addition of one straw affect the structure's resistance to shear stress?

2. Apply a shear stress to the upright square by pushing on it in the direction shown by the arrow. How resistant is the square to shear forces?

3. Next, add one more straw as shown in Figure 9b. This diagonal straw converts the square to two triangles. Apply a shear force to the same point as before.

   How has the addition of this single straw changed the structure's resistance to shear force? Why do you think triangles are so important in architecture and construction?

4. Using soda straws, pins, and masking tape (to cover sharp ends of pins), you can build a tetrahedron (a four-sided structure) like the one shown in Figure 10.

Figure 10.

Build a tetrahedron from soda straws, pins, and masking tape (to cover the pins' sharp edges). Test this structure for all types of stress.

Results and Conclusions

Do you think a tetrahedron will be resistant to compression? Do you think it will be resistant to tension? To shear? To torsional shear? What makes you think so? Figure 5d shows how to apply shear and torsional shear.

Test the tetrahedron for all types of stress. Were your predictions correct?

💡 Science Project Ideas

- Using what you have learned about the various stresses on structures, what is the tallest tower you can build using soda straws, pins, and masking tape (to cover the sharp tips of pins).

- Why are the tall antennas used to send radio waves supported by strong cables or wires?

- Using what you have learned about stresses, what is the strongest model bridge you can build from strips of cardboard, paper fasteners, string, and glue?

EXPERIMENT 2.4

Tension and Liquids: Holding Together

Question:

Is the surface of water under tension?

Hypothesis:

Yes. This skin-like tension is seen when you place a very light object on the surface of water.

Materials:

- dinner fork
- sewing needle or paper clip
- clean water
- container wider than the sewing needle or paper clip
- small piece of soap
- plastic vial or medicine cup
- eyedropper
- waxed paper
- aluminum foil
- glass
- plastic wrap

The cohesive forces between the molecules of a liquid produce tension on the liquid's surface. This phenomenon is known as surface tension. As Figure 11a shows, a molecule below the surface of a liquid is pulled equally in all directions. However, the resulting force on surface molecules is inward.

The effect of this inward force on surface molecules causes the liquid to contract, creating a skin-like effect. As a result, drops of liquids take on a spherical shape because the molecules pull together as much as is possible. For any given volume, the shape with the least surface area is a sphere.

You can see for yourself that the surface of water is really under tension.

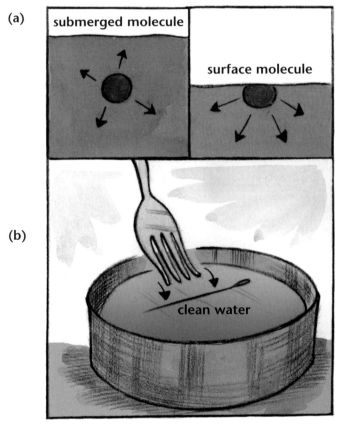

Figure 11.

a) A molecule within the volume of a liquid is pulled equally in all directions. There is no net force on it. But a molecule on the surface is pulled inward creating tension and a skin-like cover.

b) To see the tension on a surface, use a dinner fork to place a needle or paper clip on the surface of some water.

Procedure:

1. Use a dinner fork, as shown in Figure 11b, to carefully place a sewing needle or a paper clip on the surface of some clean water.

   Notice how the water surface bends like a skin as the needle or paper clip rests on its surface. The bending produces a tension similar to the tension on the top of the meterstick you used in Experiment 2.2. What happens when you carefully touch the water with a small piece of soap?

2. Fill a plastic vial or medicine cup to the brim with water. Then use an eyedropper to add water drop by drop to the vial or cup.

   Notice how the water heaps up above the top of the container. How many drops can you add before the water's weight overcomes the water's cohesive forces?

3. Again, heap some water above the top of the cup or vial. Then gently tap the side of the vessel with the eyedropper. Notice how the heaped up water holds together and shakes like jelly.

4. Once more, heap water well above the top of a medicine cup or vial. What happens when you carefully touch the water with a piece of soap? What does this tell you about the surface tension of soapy water as compared with pure water?

5. Here is another way to see the skin-like property of water. Use an eyedropper to place drops of water on a sheet of waxed paper. Do the drops spread out over the paper or do they form semi-spherical shapes? To see the cohesive forces of water, place one drop of water on waxed paper. Then place another drop very close to the first one. If necessary, add more to the second drop until the two drops just touch.

Results and Conclusions

Notice how the drops pull together to form a single drop. To see how adhesive and cohesive forces interact, place drops of water on a variety of surfaces. You might use aluminum foil, glass, and plastic wrap as well as waxed paper. What do you conclude? Which surface shows the greatest adhesion with water?

💡 Science Project Ideas

- Using mathematics, show that for any given volume, a sphere has the smallest surface.

- Try heaping other liquids in a medicine cup or vial. You might try water, rubbing alcohol, soapy water, and cooking oil. Which liquid or liquids have the strongest surface tension? Which have weak surface tension? Predict the comparative appearance of drops of these different liquids on a sheet of waxed paper. Then try it. Were your predictions correct?

- Design and carry out an experiment to measure the volume of a water drop. How do you think the volume of a water drop will compare with the volume of drops of alcohol and soapy water? Carry out experiments to test your predictions.

EXPERIMENT 2.5

Tension and Liquids: The Breaking Point

Question:

Can you measure the tension of a liquid?

Hypothesis:

You can measure the tension on a thin liquid film that is stretched to the breaking point.

Materials:

- paper clips
- thread
- water
- clean container to hold water
- milligram weights, or eyedropper, graduated cylinder, and water
- alcohol
- soapy water
- clay
- equal-arm balance or make one from stiff cardboard using a 30-cm (1-ft) ruler, scissors, pencil, finishing nail, paper clips, two cans, thread, and a Styrofoam cup

The tension on a liquid film is usually measured in grams-weight per centimeter.

Procedure:

1. Obtain an equal arm balance. If you do not have such a balance, you can easily make one as shown in Figure 12b. Place a 30-cm (1-ft) ruler on a piece of stiff cardboard. With a pencil, mark the outline of the ruler on the cardboard.

2. Use scissors to cut out the outline from the cardboard. This will become your balance beam. Draw a vertical line across the exact center of the cardboard. Make a mark slightly above the midpoint of the cardboard as shown. Make an additional mark at each end of the beam. These marks should be 1 cm above the bottom of the beam and 1 cm in from the end of the beam.

3. Push a finishing nail through the marks at the ends of the beam. Push the same finishing nail through the center mark and leave it in place. The nail will serve as the beam's fulcrum, about which it will turn.

4. Place an opened paper clip through the hole at each end of the balance beam. Place the ends of the fulcrum (nail) on two cans as shown in Figure 12c. Use thread to hang the lower third of a Styrofoam cup from the paper clip at the left end of the beam. The cup will serve as a balance pan. This completes the equal-arm balance.

5. To measure tension on a liquid film you can cut and bend a paper clip to form the three-sided frame shown in Figure 12a. Use a piece of thread to attach the frame to one end of an equal-arm balance.

6. Attach the three-sided metal frame to the paper clip on the right side. If the beam does not balance, move a piece of clay along the light end of the beam until the beam balances.

7. To measure water's surface tension, place a container of water under the right side of the beam. The frame should be submerged in the water. Now find how much weight must be added to the pan on the other side of the balance to pull the frame from the water.

Figure 12.

(a)

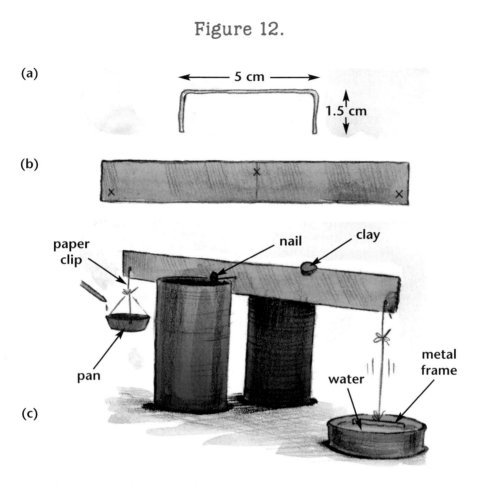

(b)

(c)

a) Make a three-sided frame of the dimensions shown by cutting and bending a paper clip.
b) The marks at the middle and ends of the beam are indicated by Xs.
c) The assembled balance is shown with the wire frame in water.

You will see the water surface stretch as it is pulled upward. The force needed will probably be quite small. If you have small weights, as small as 10, 20, 50, and 100 milligrams, you can use those. If not, you can add drops of water to the Styrofoam pan with an eyedropper.

8. To find the weight of one drop, count the number of drops needed to fill a graduated cylinder to the 10-mL mark. Then remember that one milliliter of water weighs one gram. How much does a drop of water weigh?

Results and Conclusions

How can you be certain that you are measuring surface tension? Remember, surface tension is caused by water's cohesion, the tendency of its molecules to hold together. You need to be sure you are measuring a cohesive force, not the adhesive force between the water and the metal frame. You can find out by looking at the surface of the frame after it is pulled from the water. If water remains on the frame, it must have been the water that pulled apart. If the frame is dry, the adhesive force between water and metal broke before the cohesive force between water molecules. So if the frame is dry, you are measuring the adhesive force between water and frame.

How much weight must be added to the pan to pull the frame from the water? What is water's surface tension in terms of weight per length (force per length)? You can find the surface tension by dividing the weight added to the pan by twice the length of the frame. It is twice the length of the frame because there are two surfaces (sides) to the film of water that is stretched.

Suppose, for example, that it takes 1.0 g to pull the frame off the water and the length of the frame is 5 cm. The surface tension would then be:

$$1.0 \text{ g-wt} \div 2 \times 5 \text{ cm} = 0.1 \text{ g-wt/cm}$$

What is the surface tension of water according to your measurements?

Do you think the surface tension of alcohol and soapy water will be more or less than that of water? Carry out experiments to test your prediction. Were you right? What is the surface tension of alcohol according to your measurements? What is the surface tension of soapy water?

EXPERIMENT 2.6

Elasticity and Collisions

Question:

What affects how balls bounce?

Hypothesis:

The ball's elasticity and the hardness of the surface on which it is dropped affect its bounce.

Materials:

- Superball
- a friend
- meterstick or yardstick
- hard floor or sidewalk
- surfaces such as wood, concrete, tile, macadam, carpet, grass, and soil
- pen or pencil
- notebook
- balls of Styrofoam and clay ball as well as those used in baseball, softball, tennis, basketball, lacrosse, soccer, and golf

Figure 13.

How high does a Superball
bounce when dropped from
a height of one meter?

Moving objects often bump into one another. This is true of the tiny molecules of air moving at average speeds of 1,770 kilometers per hour (1,100 mph) as well as people and cars moving at much slower speeds. It is less true of the objects that move through space, such as meteoroids, comets, planets, moons, and stars. But the craters on the moon and the remains of meteoroids that have struck Earth demonstrate that celestial objects do bump into each other from time to time.

Bumping molecules and bumping people or cars are very different. Collisions between molecules and atoms are usually elastic. Collisions between automobiles or people who bump into one another are either inelastic or only partially elastic.

During elastic collisions, no motion energy is lost. During an inelastic collision, all the energy of motion is converted to heat. For example, imagine that a car rolls down a hill and collides with a tree. After the collision, the car has lost all its motion energy and the tree is still at rest; the collision was inelastic.

In this experiment you will investigate the collision of different kinds of balls with different surfaces fixed to the earth. These collisions vary from nearly elastic to inelastic. You might begin with a Superball, which is made from a very elastic type of matter.

Procedure:

1. To test a Superball's elasticity, ask a friend to hold a meterstick or yardstick upright on a hard floor or sidewalk as shown in Figure 13. Hold the Superball so that the bottom of the ball is level with the top of the measuring stick.

2. Then drop the ball. Have your friend watch to see how high the bottom of the ball bounces after it hits the floor or sidewalk.

   Repeat the experiment several times. Does the ball bounce to very nearly the same height each time? Record the average height to which the Superball bounces in your notebook. Also record the fraction of its original height to which it bounces. If, for example, you drop it from 100 cm (1 m) and it bounces up to 90 cm, then it reached 0.9 ($\frac{9}{10}$) of its original height.

3. Repeat the experiment with a variety of other balls and record all your results. You might try a Styrofoam ball and a clay ball as well as balls used in different sports such as baseball, softball, tennis, basketball, lacrosse, soccer, and golf.

Results and Conclusions

To what fraction of the drop height does each ball rise after bouncing? How does the "bounciness" of each of these balls compare with the bounciness of a Superball?

Does the surface onto which you drop a ball affect the height to which it rises after bouncing? To find out, drop a Superball and several other balls used in games onto different surfaces such as wood, concrete, tile, macadam, carpet, grass, and soil. What do you find?

Science Project Ideas

- Design and carry out an experiment to see if there is a relationship between the height to which a ball bounces and the number of previous bounces it has made after being dropped.

- Design and carry out another experiment to see if the temperature of different balls has any effect on their bounciness.

- Investigate the meaning of elastic and inelastic collisions. How are they related to the bounciness of the different balls you tested? Are any of the bounces elastic? Are any inelastic?

CHAPTER 3

Density: A Property of All Matter

As you saw in Experiment 1.1, you can apply compression forces to a liquid provided it is in a closed container. Outside a closed container the liquid will simply spread out over a larger area. But, as you discovered, water, when contained, is practically incompressible. The same is true of all liquids.

All matter, whether solid, liquid, or gas, has a property we call density. It is a measure of the "compactness" of matter. As you might guess, solids and liquids, since they are compact, are more dense than gases, in which the molecules are far apart.

◄ Although ice is a solid, it is less dense than water, and therefore floats. Water is at its densest when at 4°C (40°F).

EXPERIMENT 3.1

Measuring the Density of Solids and Liquids

Question:

How do you calculate the density of objects?

Hypothesis:

Density can be calculated by measuring an object's volume and weight.

Materials:

- wood block, such as a toy block or a short length of a 2-in-x-4-in board
- ruler
- a balance to weigh solids and liquids
- graduated cylinder or metric measuring cup
- cooking oil
- a stone that will fit inside the graduated cylinder
- water
- rubbing alcohol
- salt water
- cup and other containers

If someone says that lead is heavier than water, you can disagree. You might say, "Do you mean a lead BB weighs more than a liter of water?" That person will probably realize his error and respond, "No, but lead will weigh more than an equal volume of water."

Density, the compactness of matter, is a measure of heaviness per volume; that is, the mass or weight per volume. You can easily find the density of a wood block.

Procedure:

1. Use a ruler to find the length, width, and height of the block in centimeters. The volume, in cubic centimeters (cm^3), will be the length times the width times the height.

2. Weigh the block. The mass (weight), in grams (g), can be obtained by using a balance.

   What is the density of your block of wood? Suppose the block is 5 cm x 10 cm x 20 cm and weighs 600 g. Its volume then is:

$$5 \text{ cm} \times 10 \text{ cm} \times 20 \text{ cm} = 1,000 \text{ cm}^3$$

   Its density is:

$$600 \text{ g} \div 1,000 \text{ cm}^3 = 0.60 \text{ g/cm}^3$$

Results and Conclusions

Finding the density of a solid is simple if its dimensions are easily measured. But suppose you want to know the density of a stone. Most stones have an irregular shape, but you can still find the density of such an object.

Procedure:

1. Find a stone that will fit inside a graduated cylinder or metric measuring cup. Weigh the stone and record its mass (weight).

2. Then fill the graduated cylinder about halfway with water. Read the water level in the cylinder and record the volume occupied by the water.

3. Next, add the stone. It will displace a volume of water equal to its own volume. Record the new volume indicated by the water level. The graduated cylinder may measure volume in milliliters (mL). This is not a problem, however, because a milliliter and a cubic centimeter have the same volume. Consequently, you can substitute cubic centimeters for milliliters.

4. Use the data you have recorded to obtain the volume of the stone. Then determine its density. Is the stone more or less dense than the wood? How can you use the same graduated cylinder and the balance to find the density of water? What do you find the density of water to be? Is it more or less dense than wood? Is it more or less dense than the stone? Will the stone float in water? Will the wood float in water?

Results and Conclusions

What tentative conclusion can you draw about a solid's density and whether or not it will float in water? Find the density of some cooking oil in grams per milliliter. Do you think the oil will sink or float when added to water? Try it! Were you right?

What is the density of rubbing alcohol? Is it more or less dense than water? Why does it not sink or float in water? Prepare a saturated solution of salt water by dissolving as much salt as possible in a cup of water. What is the density of the salt water? Do you think water from the ocean will be more or less dense than pure water? What makes you think so?

 Science Project Ideas

- Measure the density of a number of different solids and liquids. What is the most dense solid you measured? The least dense? What is the most dense liquid you measured? The least dense? Which solids do you predict will float in water? Which do you think will sink in water?

- Design and carry out an experiment to find the density of sand. Remember: The sand particles have air between them.

EXPERIMENT 3.2

Comparing the Densities of Liquids

Question:

Can you compare the densities of different liquids?

Hypothesis:

Yes. You can color different liquids, mix them, and see which ones sink.

Materials:

- salt, preferably kosher salt
- a balance for weighing
- tablespoon
- containers
- graduated cylinder or measuring cup
- water
- green, red, and blue food coloring
- 4 clear pill vials or medicine cups
- kitchen counter
- medicine dropper

In the previous experiment you found that alcohol was less dense than water. However, alcohol did not float on water because it dissolves in water. But there is a way to compare the densities of even those liquids that are soluble in one another.

Procedure:

1. Make a saturated salt solution by adding 60 to 70 grams (7 to 8 table-spoons) of kosher salt to 200 mL (7 oz) of water. Continue to add salt, if necessary, until no more will dissolve.

   If possible, use kosher salt. Ordinary table salt has added ingredients that make solutions cloudy. You will probably need 13 to 17 tablespoons of kosher salt to make a saturated solution in 200 mL (7 oz) of water.

2. Pour the saturated solution into another container to separate it from any undissolved salt.

3. Then pour *half* the saturated solution (about 100 mL, or 3½ oz) into a second container. Dilute this portion by adding to it 100 mL (3½ oz) of water.

4. Pour half of this diluted solution into a third container. Dilute this liquid by adding 100 mL (3½ oz) of water.

   You now have three solutions. The first is a saturated salt solution; the second has half as much salt per milliliter as the first; the third has one-fourth as much salt per volume as the first.

5. To enable you to identify these different solutions, add a few drops of green food coloring to the first solution. Then add a few drops of red food coloring to the second, and a few drops of blue food coloring to the third and least concentrated solution.

6. Next, place four clear pill vials or medicine cups side by side on a kitchen counter. Fill the first vial about three fourths of the way with the green (saturated) solution. In a similar way, pour some red solution into the second vial and some blue solution into the third vial. Add plain water to the fourth vial.

7. Using a medicine dropper, remove some of the red solution from the second vial. Place the tip of the dropper in the middle of the water in the fourth vial. *Gently* squeeze a little of the red solution out into the water, as shown in Figure 14. Does the red liquid sink or rise in the water?

8. Repeat the experiment in the blue liquid. Does the red liquid rise or sink when it is squeezed gently into the blue solution? What happens when you squeeze a drop of red liquid into the green liquid? Does it rise or sink?

   What happens when you gently squeeze a drop of green solution into each of the other three liquids? When you squeeze drops of the blue solution in the other liquids? In which liquids does the blue liquid sink? In which one(s) does it rise?

Figure 14.

plain
water

Does the drop of red liquid float or sink in the clear water?

Results and Conclusions

Try to predict what will happen when you squeeze a little water from the fourth vial into each of the other three liquids. Were your predictions correct? Which of these four liquids do you think is most dense? Check your prediction by weighing 50 mL (2 oz) of each liquid.

Save your colored liquids for the next experiment.

Science Project Ideas

- Design and carry out an experiment to compare the densities of hot and cold water. Which one is denser?

- What observations and measurements can you make to show that hot air is less dense than cold air?

EXPERIMENT 3.3

Comparing Densities Using Liquid Layers

Question:

If liquids of different densities are combined, will they appear in layers?

Hypothesis:

You can layer liquids of different densities by using a transparent soda straw.

Materials:

- transparent plastic soda straws
- vials of the green, red, blue, and clear liquids you prepared in Experiment 3.2
- clear vials or medicine cups
- rubbing alcohol
- water
- cooking oil
- other liquids such as cranberry juice, apple juice, vinegar, salad oil, syrup, grape juice
- pen
- paper
- eyedropper

Pipettes are used by chemists to pick up and move liquids. But you can use a soda straw for the same purpose. And, with a clear plastic soda straw, you can make layers of liquids that have different densities.

Procedure:

1. To see how a soda straw can be used to lift liquids, place a straw in some water. Place your index finger on the top end of the straw as shown in Figure 15.

Figure 15.

You can make a soda straw pipette, use it to pick up liquids, and make liquid layers.

2. Then lift the straw from the water. Air pressure, which you will investigate in the next chapter, holds the water in the straw.

3. Lift your finger and the water will flow out of the straw.

   Once you are good at moving liquids with your see-through straw, you can make layers of different colored liquids in the straw. To make two layers, dip the straw a short way into a vial of the blue liquid you prepared in the previous experiment.

4. Put your finger over the straw and lift it out of the liquid. Keeping your finger on top of the straw, place the straw in the red solution.

5. Push the straw deep enough into the liquid so that the blue liquid in the straw is lower than the surface of the red liquid in the vial. Then release your finger. Red liquid will enter the straw, pushing the blue liquid upward until it is even with the surface of the red liquid in the vial.

6. Put your finger back on the top of the straw again and lift the straw out of the red liquid. You have made a two-layered, liquid "cake" with blue on top of red.

Results and Conclusions

Why can't you make a two-layered cake with red on top of blue? How many two-layered cakes can you make from the four liquids? How many three-layered cakes can you prepare? Can you make a four-layered cake?

Add vials of rubbing alcohol and cooking oil so that you now have six different liquids. How many two-, three-, and four-layered cakes can you make from these six liquids? Can you make five-layered cakes? How many? Can you make a six-layered cake? Which liquid is always the top layer? Which liquid is always the bottom layer?

Based on this experiment, list the six liquids according to their densities. Put the least dense liquid at the top of the list and the most dense liquid at the bottom of the list.

Using liquid layers in a straw, see if you can add some of the following liquids to your density list: cranberry juice, apple juice, vinegar, salad oil, syrup, and grape juice.

What do you think will happen if you make a two-layered cake and then turn the straw upside down? Will the layers remain separated? Try it! What happened? What do you think will happen when you turn the straw right side up again?

From what you have learned, make liquid layers in a vial or medicine cup using an eyedropper to move the liquids.

EXPERIMENT 3.4

Density of a Gas

Question:
Can you measure the density of a gas?

Hypothesis:
Yes. You can weigh the substances that produce the gas before and after the gas is made.

Materials:
- seltzer tablet
- balance you built in Experiment 2.5
- twistie
- clay
- test tube
- graduated cylinder or metric measuring cup
- water
- heavy drinking glass
- pen or pencil
- notebook
- plastic pail
- rubber tubing (about 50 cm [20 in] long)
- one-hole rubber stopper to fit test tube
- glass tube about 10 cm (4 in) long to fit into rubber stopper
- large bottle (500 mL– 1 L [1 pint–1 quart])
- square piece of cardboard or glass to cover mouth of bottle

Carbon dioxide is not very soluble in water. Furthermore, the substances that react to form this gas can be weighed before and after the gas is produced. As a result, the density of carbon dioxide can be found by making two weighings and measuring a volume.

You will weigh some water and a seltzer tablet before and after they react. When they react, carbon dioxide gas will form and escape. Any loss of weight must be due to the carbon dioxide gas that you will collect in a separate container. Having collected the carbon dioxide, you can measure its volume. Knowing its weight and volume, you can easily calculate its density.

Procedure:

1. Break a seltzer tablet in half. Place the two pieces on the pan of the balance.

2. Also use clay to stand a test tube holding about 10 mL of water upright on the balance pan as shown in Figure 16a. The test tube should be about one-quarter to one-third full. Record the total mass of tablet, clay, and test tube.

3. Next, set up the apparatus shown in Figure 16b. The test tube can be supported by a drinking glass. Fill the large bottle with water. Fill the pail about one third of the way with water.

4. Cover the mouth of the bottle with a glass or cardboard square. Holding the square against the bottle, turn it upside down. Then put the mouth of the bottle below the water level in the pail.

5. Place the unconnected end of the rubber tubing inside and at the top of the large bottle of water. Drop the two pieces of seltzer tablet into the water in the test tube and immediately insert the one-hole rubber stopper into the mouth of the test tube.

Figure 16.

(a)

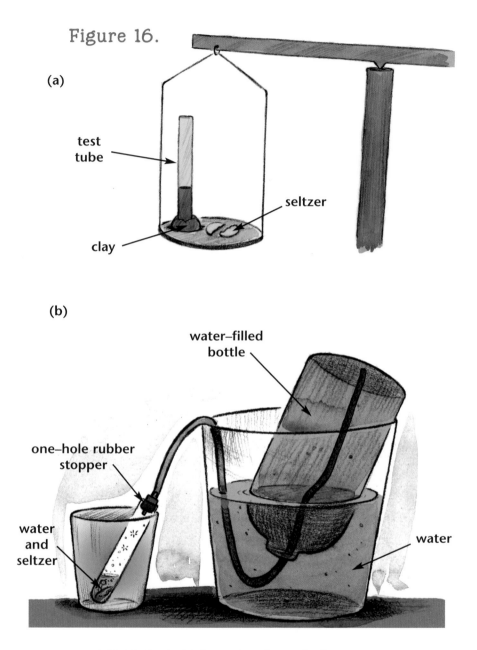

test
tube

seltzer

clay

(b)

water–filled
bottle

one–hole rubber
stopper

water
and
seltzer

water

a) Weigh the test tube, water, clay, and seltzer.
b) The apparatus for collecting the carbon dioxide
   formed when the seltzer reacts with water is shown.

Carbon dioxide gas will be produced and escape through the glass and rubber tubing that connects the test tube to the large bottle. There it will collect while displacing water from the bottle. After about ten minutes, the reaction will be nearly complete.

6. Remove the rubber tubing from the bottle and place the tubing outside the pail. Then cover the mouth of the bottle with a square piece of cardboard or glass and remove it from the pail.

7. Use a graduated cylinder or metric measuring cup to find the volume of gas that was produced by refilling the bottle. Reweigh the test tube and water. Again, the clay can be used to hold the test tube upright on the balance pan.

Results and Conclusions

How can you find the mass of the carbon dioxide that was produced in the test tube and then collected in the bottle? Record your data in a notebook.

From the mass of the gas and its volume, determine the density of the carbon dioxide. What assumptions have you made in finding the density of carbon dioxide?

 Science Project Idea

- Design and, under adult supervision, carry out experiments to find the density of other gases such as air, oxygen, hydrogen, nitrogen, or neon.

CHAPTER 4

Pressure, Buoyancy, and Archimedes

A ll forms of matter can produce pressure, which is defined as force per area. Even air exerts a pressure. Like all matter, air is pulled toward Earth by gravity. The weight of a column of air extending all the way from Earth's surface to the top of the atmosphere is significant. In fact, we can measure the pressure exerted by air with a barometer. It is about 10 newtons (1.02 kg-wt) per square centimeter, or 14.7 pounds per square inch. A pressure this great will force a column of mercury in a tube to a height of 76 cm (30 in) or a column of water to a height of 10.3 m (34 ft).

◀ A barometer measures air pressure. If the barometer is rising and air pressure is high, the weather will be dry and fair. Falling air pressure is an indication of stormy, wet weather.

EXPERIMENT 4.1

The Meaning of Pressure

Question:

Do different shapes create different force per area when the same amount of pressure is applied to them?

Hypothesis:

The same pressure applied to materials of different shapes will result in differences in force per area.

Materials:

- wooden dowels with different diameters
- clay
- heavy book or brick
- nail or sharp pencil
- balance
- ruler

As you learned on the previous page, pressure is defined as force per area. To understand what this means, obtain a number of wooden dowels with different diameters.

Procedure:

1. Place the dowels on lumps of clay as shown in Figure 17.

2. Then, put a weight such as a heavy book or a brick on top of each dowel. Which dowel sinks deepest into the clay? Which dowel has the smallest diameter? The bottom of which dowel has the smallest area?

3. Replace one of the dowels with a nail or a sharp pencil. How far do you predict this object will sink into the clay? Try it! Were you right?

Results and Conclusions

Weigh the book or the brick and calculate the actual pressure that was exerted on the clay under each dowel. For example, suppose the brick weighed 2 kg and the dowel on which it rested had a diameter of 2.0 cm. The force (weight) pushing down on the dowel was 2 kilograms-weight (kg-wt) or 19.6 newtons (N). (The weight of a 1.0 kg mass is 9.8 N.) The area of the end of the dowel, which is a circle, would be:

$$\pi r^2 = 3.14 \times (1 \text{ cm})^2 = 3.14 \text{ cm}^2$$

The pressure (P) would be the force (F) per area (A), which would be:

$$P = F \div A = 2 \text{ kg-wt} \div 3.14 \text{ cm}^2 = 0.64 \text{ kg-wt/cm}^2$$

or

$$P = F \div A = 19.6 \text{ N} \div 3.14 \text{ cm}^2 = 6.24 \text{ N/cm}^2$$

Therefore, the pressure exerted by the end of the dowel is 0.64 kg-wt/cm² or 6.24 N/cm².

Figure 17.

If a brick is placed on each dowel, which dowel will sink deepest into the clay? Where will the pressure be greatest?

EXPERIMENT 4.2

Air Pressure

Question:

How can you measure air pressure?

Hypothesis:

Air pressure can be measured by how high it forces a contained liquid to rise.

Materials:

- large test tube or long tube sealed at one end
- water
- pan
- aneroid barometer
- mountain or high hill
- notebook
- pen or pencil
- automobile or bus
- elevator
- building with several flights of stairs

We live at the bottom of a great sea of air that stretches upward some 120 km (75 mi). However, all but one percent of that air is found within 32 km (20 mi) of Earth's surface. The weight of the air creates a pressure that we can measure with a barometer. The great seventeenth-century Italian scientist, Evangelista Torricelli, was the first person to measure air pressure.

(a)   (b)   **Figure 18.**

vacuum

76 cm

mercury

water

Remove your finger
and water will stay
in tube.

a) Torricelli's mercury barometer showed that at sea level air pressure can
   equal that of a column of mercury 76 cm high.
b) Air pressure can hold up other liquids as well. You can see a similar effect
   with water.

Torricelli made a narrow glass tube about 1.2 m (4 ft) long sealed at
one end. He then filled it with mercury. Placing his finger over the open
end, he placed that end in a dish of mercury and slowly raised the tube
until it was vertical. When he had finished, he could see that the level of
the mercury in the tube was about 76 cm (30 in) above the mercury in the
dish as shown in Figure 18a. He correctly reasoned that the pressure of the
air must be able to support a column of mercury 76 cm (30 in) high.

You can see for yourself that air pressure can hold up a column of liquid.

Procedure:

1. Fill with water a test tube or a long tube that is sealed at one end.

2. Put your finger over the open end of the tube, turn the tube upside down, then put the tube in a pan of water as shown in Figure 18b.

3. Remove your finger. Does the water remain in the tube?

Results and Conclusions

When you removed your finger, the water stayed in the tube. This shows that air pressure can hold up a column of liquid, in this case, water. Mercury is 13.5 times as dense as water. So Torricelli reasoned that the atmosphere could support a column of water 13.5 times as high as a column of mercury, or 10.26 m (33.6 ft). His prediction was later confirmed by another experiment.

In building his mercury device, which came to be known as a barometer, he also created a vacuum in this device. When the mercury level fell from 1.2 m to 0.76 m, nothing replaced the mercury that had been at the high end of the tube. Therefore, the space at the top of the inverted tube was completely empty, a true vacuum (except for tiny amounts of mercury vapor).

Mercury is poisonous and you should not touch it or breathe its fumes. But you can measure air pressure with an aneroid barometer. An aneroid barometer (Figure 19a) has a hole in the back where air can enter. The air pushes against a sealed, thin, round, hollow metal can from which most of the air has been removed. The outside of the can is attached to a spring. A series of levers connects the spring to a chain that turns a pointer over the dial of the barometer as shown in Figure 19b.

When air pressure increases, the sides of the can are pushed inward, stretching the spring. The spring pulls on the chain turning the pointer so that it points toward a larger number on the dial. When air pressure decreases, the sides of the can move outward, the spring is under less tension so the pointer lies above a smaller number on the dial.

What do you think will happen to the air pressure as you ascend a mountain or a high hill?

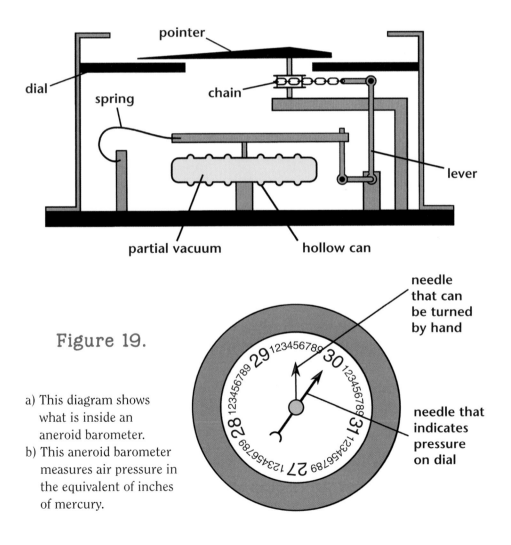

Figure 19.

a) This diagram shows what is inside an aneroid barometer.
b) This aneroid barometer measures air pressure in the equivalent of inches of mercury.

Procedure:

1. To check your prediction, record the pressure on an aneroid barometer at the bottom of the hill or mountain.

2. Then carry the barometer to the top of the hill or mountain. Again, record the barometric pressure. Has the pressure changed? Was your prediction correct?

3. Take the barometer with you on an automobile or bus ride. Does air pressure change as you go up and down hills? Can you feel the effects of pressure changes in your ears?

4. Is there a change in air pressure as you go up and down in an elevator? Can you detect any change in pressure when you climb a flight of stairs? Can you detect any change when you climb several flights of stairs?

Results and Conclusions

Air pressure is lower at higher elevations, and higher at lower elevations.

Is the upward pressure of the air the same as the downward and sideways pressure? To find out, turn the barometer so that the small hole in its back faces upward, then downward, and then sideways. Read the barometer in each position. What do you conclude?

Science Project Ideas

- Under adult supervision, design and carry out an experiment to show that air pressure can support a column of water about 10 m (33 ft) high.

- Why do the dials on household aneroid barometers seldom go below 26 (inches of mercury) or above 32?

EXPERIMENT 4.3

A Simple Barometer

Question:

Can you make a simple barometer?

Hypothesis:

Yes, you can build a barometer that can be controlled by the pressure of your own breath.

Materials:

- **an adult**
- large test tube
- water
- food coloring
- soap
- clear, flexible plastic tubing
- rubber bands
- tape
- indoor wall or post
- one-hole rubber stopper that fits the test tube
- short piece of glass tubing or rigid plastic tubing

You can make a simple barometer like the one shown in Figure 20. It will show changes in atmospheric pressure.

Procedure:

1. To begin, fill a large test tube about two thirds of the way with some water to which you have added a drop or two of food coloring.

2. Find a one-hole rubber stopper that fits the test tube.

3. **Ask an adult** to wet a short piece of glass tubing or rigid plastic tubing with some soap and insert it into the rubber stopper.

4. Attach a length of clear plastic tubing to the short piece of tubing. Invert the test tube. Then fasten the tubing to the test tube with rubber bands.

5. Gently blow air into the end of the tubing to force some water from the test tube into the tubing.

6. Use tape to attach the barometer you have made to an indoor wall or post.

7. To see the effect of increased pressure, blow air gently into the end of the tubing. To see the effect of a decrease in air pressure, gently suck a little air from the tubing.

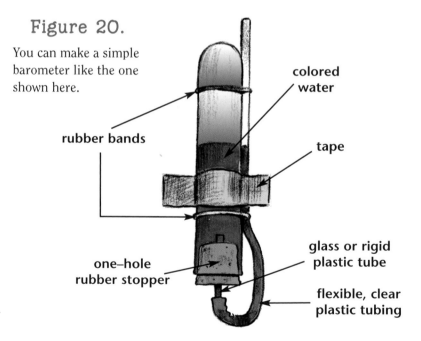

Figure 20.

You can make a simple barometer like the one shown here.

colored water

rubber bands

tape

one–hole rubber stopper

glass or rigid plastic tube

flexible, clear plastic tubing

Results and Conclusions

What is the major fault with the barometer you have made? What happens when you hold a warm cloth against the test tube?

EXPERIMENT 4.4

Water Pressure

Question:

Does water pressure function the same way as air pressure?

Hypothesis:

Yes, water pressure is greater the deeper you go.

Materials:

- **an adult**
- aneroid barometer
- clear, self-sealing plastic bag or plastic bag and a twistie
- pail or tub filled with water
- very large can (coffee can)
- hammer
- nail
- masking tape
- sink

As you saw in the previous experiment, air pressure decreases as you ascend in the sea of air. It increases as you descend deeper into the sea of air by going down a mountain, an elevator, or several flights of stairs. What do you think will happen to the pressure as you go deeper in water? You can use your aneroid barometer to find out.

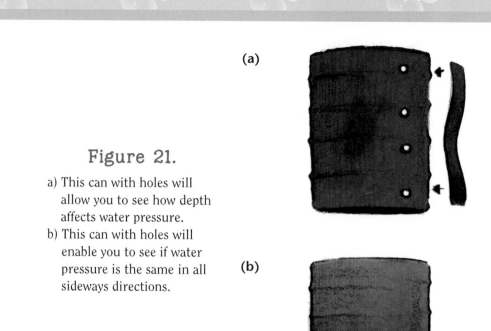

(a)

Figure 21.

a) This can with holes will allow you to see how depth affects water pressure.

b) This can with holes will enable you to see if water pressure is the same in all sideways directions.

(b)

Procedure:

1. Put the barometer in a clear, self-sealing plastic bag or one you can seal with a twistie.

2. Slowly lower the enclosed barometer into a pail or tub filled with water. What happens to the pressure as you lower the barometer deeper into the water?

   Here is another way to see how pressure is affected by the depth of water.

3. **Ask an adult** to help you punch holes of equal diameter in the sides of a very large can using a hammer and nail. Make one hole near the bottom of the can, another near the top, and two in between as shown in Figure 21a. Cover the holes with masking tape.

4. Take the can outside or near a sink and fill it with water.

5. Have a friend hold the can well above the ground while you quickly remove the tape from the holes. From which hole does the water project farthest? What does this experiment tell you about pressure as you go deeper in water?

6. Next, add three more equally spaced holes to match the one already near the bottom of the can. Again, cover the holes with tape and then fill the can with water. Hold the can outside or over a sink. Have someone quickly remove the tape.

Results and Conclusions

How does the projection of water from each hole compare? What can you say about the pressure at the same depth in water? Does the pressure appear to be equal in all directions? (See Figure 21b.)

💡 Science Project Ideas

- Carry out an experiment to show that water pressure is proportional to the depth of the water; that is, doubling the depth doubles the pressure, tripling the depth triples the pressure, and so on.

- Design and carry out an experiment to show that at the same depth water pressure is equal in all directions, up, down, and sideways.

- What are siphons? Develop a demonstration to show how they work.

EXPERIMENT 4.5

Amazing Effects of Air Pressure

Question:

Can you show the effects of air pressure?

Hypothesis:

You can show air-pressure effects by performing a few simple demonstrations.

Materials:

- **an adult**
- empty 1-gallon metal can
- soap and water
- cup
- stove or hot plate
- tongs or gloves
- insulated mat or newspapers
- cap for can or large rubber stopper
- towel
- cold water
- test tube or vial
- paper towel
- a sink
- clear plastic soda straw
- a glass
- small finishing nail
- pint-size plastic soda bottle with screw-on cap
- pliers
- funnel
- bottle
- clay
- paper clip
- 2 suction cups about 2 inches in diameter

Air Pressure Can Crush an Empty Can

Procedure:

1. Find an empty 1-gallon metal can. Clean the inside thoroughly with soap and water. Then pour a cup of water into the can. Leave the opening into the can uncovered.

2. **Ask an adult** to put the can on a stove burner or hot plate. After the water in the can has boiled for several minutes and filled the can with steam, **have the adult** use tongs or gloves to quickly place the can on an insulated mat or some newspapers.

3. **The adult** should then immediately screw the cover back on the can or plug its opening with a large rubber stopper. Then cover the can with a towel that has been soaked in cold water.

Results and Conclusions

The steam, which has replaced the air in the can, will condense as it cools, creating a partial vacuum. You will then see what happens when the pressure of the air outside the can becomes much greater than the pressure inside the can. What happens?

Air Pressure Supporting Water

Procedure:

1. Fill a test tube or vial brimful of water. Cover the mouth of the tube or vial with a small piece of paper towel.

2. Turn the vessel upside down over a sink.

Results and Conclusions

You will find that air pressure on the piece of towel keeps the water in the tube or vial. This will not work without the paper towel. What do you think is the role of the paper towel?

A Drinking Straw that Will Not Let You Drink

Procedure:

1. Use a clear plastic straw to drink water from a glass.

2. Then, with a small finishing nail, make a hole in the straw about 5 cm (2 in) below its upper end.

3. Now try to drink through the straw.

Results and Conclusions

What do you find? Can you drink through the straw if you cover the hole with your finger? Do you think you can use this straw as a pipette as you did in Experiment 3.3? Try it! Were you right?

A Leaky Bottle

Procedure:

1. Find a pint-size plastic soda bottle that has a screw-on cap. Fill it about three-fourths full with water and screw the cap on tightly.

2. Then use a small finishing nail to make a hole in the side of the bottle near its bottom. You may need pliers to force the nail through the plastic. Why does the water not empty from the bottle?

3. Next, make another small hole near the top of the bottle.

Results and Conclusions

Why do you think water now flows out of the bottle? What happens if you place your finger over the upper hole? How can you explain what happens? You might like to hold this bottle in front of a friend and see if he or she can figure out how you control the flow of water.

A Funnel That Does Not Work

Procedure:

1. Pour water into a funnel that rests on a bottle. The water runs freely through the funnel into the bottle.

2. Remove the funnel and place a ring of soft clay on the mouth of the bottle. Put the funnel back on the bottle using the clay to seal the funnel to the mouth of the bottle.

   What happens when you pour water into the funnel now? How can you explain what you observe? Open a paper clip. Gently push the wire through the clay to make a hole into the bottle.

Results and Conclusions

What happens to the water in the funnel after you make the hole so that air can leave the bottle? How do you explain what you observe?

EXPERIMENT 4.6

Pressure of Liquids, Archimedes, and Buoyancy

Question:

How can you calculate the volume of an irregularly shaped object?

Hypothesis:

The volume is calculated by measuring how much water the object displaces when submerged.

Materials:

- clay
- water
- metric measuring cup
- steel washers
- string
- pennies and other coins
- tape
- lead sinkers
- rubbing alcohol
- plastic bag
- twisties
- balance
- rubber balloon
- air pump
- yardstick
- thread
- spring scale

Procedure:

1. Make a large ball of clay around the lower end of a length of string.

2. Use a sensitive spring scale to weigh the clay. Record its weight.

3. Weigh it again when it is submerged in water as shown in Figure 22. Record its weight in water.

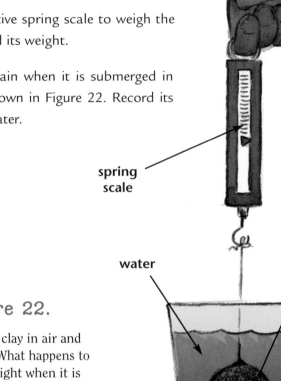

spring scale

water

clay

Figure 22.

Weigh a ball of clay in air and then in water. What happens to its apparent weight when it is placed in water?

Results and Conclusions

How much weight did the ball appear to lose when in water? (Save the clay for the next experiment.) How do you think your weight in water would compare with your weight in air?

Archimedes, a Greek philosopher who lived from 287 to 212 BC, was one of the first people to actually do experiments. One of his experiments was the one you just did.

Archimedes' king, thinking he might have been cheated, asked Archimedes to find out whether or not his crown was made of pure gold. Archimedes knew the density of gold. He weighed the crown, but how could he find the volume of such an odd-shaped object?

While sitting in his bath, Archimedes suddenly realized something you already know—a solid object will displace its own volume when submerged in a liquid. That is common knowledge today, but 2,250 years ago no one had thought of it. According to legend, Archimedes leaped from his bath and running naked through the streets shouted, "Eureka! Eureka!" which in Greek means "I have found it!"

The sudden realization that the volume of an irregularly shaped solid can be found by immersing it in a liquid led Archimedes to another discovery. It is one that you can also discover.

Procedure:

1. Find the volume, in milliliters or cubic centimeters, of the ball of clay you weighed earlier by immersing it in some water in a metric measuring cup. What volume of water does it displace? What is the volume of the clay?

2. In Experiment 3.1, you probably found that the density of water is 1.0 gram per cubic cm (or mL). Using that information, what weight of the water was displaced by the clay?

Results and Conclusions

How much weight did the clay appear to lose when weighed in water? How does the clay's loss of weight in water compare with the weight of the water it displaces?

Repeat the experiment several times using different solids. You might try a bunch of steel washers held together with thread, a stack of pennies and other coins held together with tape, and lead sinkers with different volumes. Are your results similar in each case? As accurately as your measurements allow, does a solid's loss of weight in water always equal the weight of the water displaced? Do you agree with Archimedes that *an object submerged in a fluid is buoyed up by a force equal to the weight of the fluid displaced?*

Notice that Archimedes' principle, stated above, does not specify water. It says, "buoyed up by the weight of *the fluid* displaced." This implies that his principle works with any fluid; that is, with any liquid or gas. To check this idea, repeat the experiment with clay using rubbing alcohol in place of water. What do you find?

If Archimedes' principle applies to gases, what would you expect air to weigh when weighed in air? To check your prediction, hang a plastic bag and a twistie from each end of a yardstick balance like the one shown in Figure 23. Open one bag and fill it by dragging it through the air. Then seal the bag with the twistie and suspend it from the balance again. How much does air appear to weigh? What do you conclude?

Repeat the experiment but replace the plastic bag with a rubber balloon, which you can fill with an air pump. What do you find?

The density of air at room temperature is about 1.2 grams per liter. How can you confirm this density using a balloon and applying Archimedes' principle?

Figure 23.

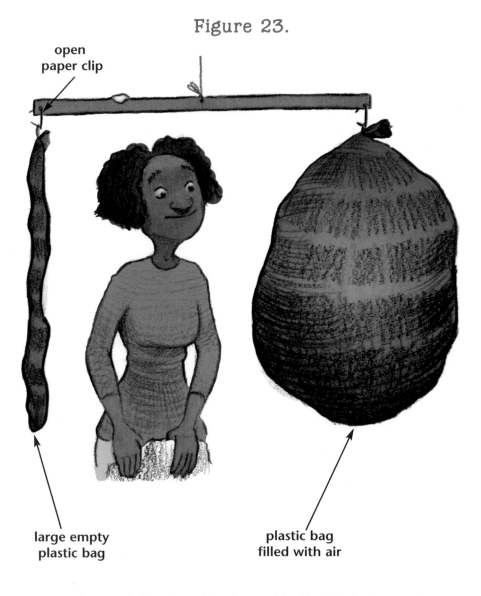

open
paper clip

large empty
plastic bag

plastic bag
filled with air

How much does air weigh when weighed in air? Find out by using the balance, plastic bags, and twisties shown here.

💡 Science Project Ideas

- Design an experiment to determine your weight while submerged in water. Then, **under adult supervision,** carry out your experiment.

- A liter (1,000 cm³) of air has a mass of 1.2 g. What is the apparent loss of mass when a 79.00-g piece of iron, which has a volume of 10 cm³, is weighed in air? How could you detect such a weight loss?

- Place an egg in a pint-size jar that is nearly filled with water. The egg sinks. Add a heaping tablespoonful of salt to the water and stir. Why does the egg now float? Can you find a way to make the egg float in the *middle* of the jar?

EXPERIMENT 4.7

Sink or Float?

Question:

Why do some objects float in water while others sink?

Hypothesis:

Objects that displace more than their weight in water will float.

Materials:

- clay
- balance
- clean, empty tuna-fish can
- metric measuring cup or graduated cylinder
- tub of water

In Chapter 3 you measured the density of a stone and a wood block among other things. You found that the wood floated in water but the stone sank. This may have suggested to you that matter more dense than water sinks in water, while matter less dense than water floats. If you tested a number of other solids, you may have found additional evidence for believing that whether an object sinks or floats in water depends on its density.

From the data you collected in Experiment 4.6, what can you predict about the density of clay? What were the weight and volume of the clay? What is the density of the clay you used?

Procedure:

1. Take that lump of clay and mold it into the shape of a boat. You will find that you can make the clay float. Remembering Archimedes' principle, what have you done to the clay to make it float? What weight of water does the clay boat displace?

   How many grams of cargo will your boat hold without sinking? The easiest cargo to add is water. And, since the density of water is 1.0 g/mL, you can easily measure out the predicted weight of the cargo. How could you change your boat so that it will hold more cargo?

2. Obtain a clean, empty tuna-fish can. How much does the can weigh? What is the outside volume of the can? Based on the data you have collected about the can, do you think it will float or sink when placed in water? Try it! Were you right?

Results and Conclusions

If the can floated, see if you can predict the maximum weight of cargo it will hold without sinking. Carefully add that amount of cargo to see if your prediction is correct. Were you right?

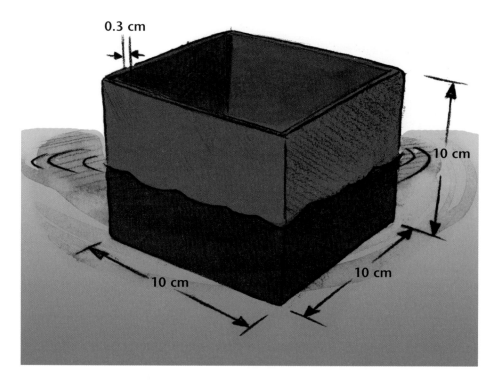

Figure 24.

Will this ill-shaped steel boat float in water?

Floating, Pressure, and Buoyancy

As you found in Experiment 4.4, water pressure increases with depth. At a depth of 10 m, the water pressure equals the pressure of the atmosphere ($10 N/cm^2$ or $1.0 kg-wt/cm^2$.) You can easily understand why the pressure of water at a depth of 10 m equals the pressure of the air. All you have to do is to consider a column of water 10 m (1,000 cm) high with a base that is 1.0 cm x 1.0 cm. The volume of this column of water is:

1.0 cm x 1.0 cm x 1,000 cm = 1,000 cm^3 or 1,000 mL

Since the density of water is 1.0 g/mL, the water weighs 1,000 g or 1.0 kg. Hence, the pressure due to that column of water is $1.0 kg-wt/cm^2$.

Of course, the total pressure at that depth is 2.0 kg-wt/cm^2 because there is also the pressure of the atmosphere, which is 1.0 kg-wt/cm^2. At twice the depth (20 m), the pressure due to water would be twice as great; at half that depth (5 m), the pressure due to water would be half as much.

To see why a steel boat can float in water, consider a "boat" made of steel that is 10 cm x 10 cm x 10 cm and only 0.3 cm thick (see Figure 24). The outside volume of the boat is:

$$10 \text{ cm} \times 10 \text{ cm} \times 10 \text{ cm} = 1{,}000 \text{ cm}^3$$

The inside volume of the boat, which is occupied by air, is:

$$9.7 \text{ cm} \times 9.7 \text{ cm} \times 9.7 \text{ cm} = 913 \text{ cm}^3$$

Therefore, the volume of steel in this ill-shaped boat is:

$$1{,}000 \text{ cm}^3 - 913 \text{ cm}^3 = 87 \text{ cm}^3$$

Since the density of steel is 7.9 g-wt/cm^3, the boat's weight is:

$$87 \text{ cm}^3 \times 7.9 \text{ g-wt/cm}^3 = 687 \text{ g-wt}$$

From Archimedes' principle, we know the boat will be buoyed up by a force equal to the weight of the water it displaces. The boat could displace 1,000 cm^3 without sinking. But it only needs to displace 687 g-wt to support its weight. Consequently, it will float. See if you can figure out how much of the boat will be above the water when it floats.

CHAPTER 5

Expansion and Contraction of Matter

If you accurately measure the density of water at different temperatures, you will find the measurements are slightly different. The density of water is 1.00 g/mL at 4.0°C (39.2°F). At 80°C (176°F), its density is 0.971 g/mL. The same is true of other liquids and of gases and solids as well. For example, the density of oxygen at 0°C (32°F) is 1.43 g/L. At 100°C (212°F), the density of oxygen is 1.04 g/L. Even the density of solids changes with temperature. At 0°C, the density of iron is 7.87 g/cm³; at 100°C, its density is 7.84 g/cm³.

In this chapter, among other things, you will find out why densities change with temperature.

◀ A propane burner is fired, heating air to make it lighter. The lighter gases will rise, inflating the hot air balloon.

EXPERIMENT 5.1

Expansion of a Solid: Getting Larger

Question:

Do the properties of metal change when heated?

Hypothesis:

Yes, metal expands and becomes less dense when heated.

Materials:

- **an adult**
- hammer
- 3-in finishing nails
- 2 wooden blocks
- 2 tables
- 2 C-clamps
- steel washer
- pencil
- rubber band
- steel and aluminum wires, each about 3 m long
- 2 friends
- matches
- 4 candles

Ask an adult to help you with this experiment. You will be working with matches and candles.

Procedure:

1. Hammer a 3-in finishing nail into one side of each of two wooden blocks.

2. Place two tables about 3 m (10 ft) apart. Fasten the blocks to the tables with C-clamps as shown in Figure 25.

3. Put one end of a 3-m (10-ft) length of steel wire through a steel washer. Wind the wire around itself several times to fasten it to the washer.

4. Use a rubber band to attach the washer to the nail in the wooden block on the left as shown in Figure 25. Bend the end of the wire downward so that it points straight down toward the block. This end of the wire will serve as a pointer.

5. Twist the other end of the long wire around the nail in the other block. Then pull the tables apart until the wire is almost straight and the rubber band is stretched. With a pencil, mark the block directly under the end of the pointer.

6 **Under adult supervision**, ask two friends to slowly move the flames of four lighted candles back and forth along the wire while you watch the pointer.

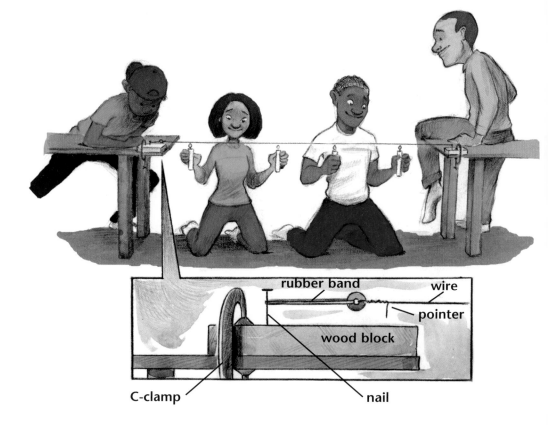

Figure 25.

Does a metal wire change in length when heated?

Results and Conclusions

Does the length of the long wire change when it gets hotter? How do you know? Does it get longer or shorter? Mark the new position of the pointer. How much did the length of the wire change? By what fraction of its original length did it change?

Under adult supervision, repeat the experiment with an aluminum wire. How did the change in length of the aluminum wire compare with that of the steel wire?

From what you have observed in this experiment, explain why the density of a metal changes when heated.

💡 Science Project Ideas

- Find a jar with a metal screw-on lid that is very tight. Let hot tap water run over the lid for a few seconds. Why is the lid much easier to open after being heated?

- Investigate some practical applications of the expansion of substances when heated. You might begin with thermometers and thermostats, but there are many more.

- What are some practical precautions that must be taken due to the fact that materials used in construction expand or contract with changes in temperature? For example, why are there spaces between sections of bridges and railroad tracks?

EXPERIMENT 5.2

Expansion of a Solid: A Detailed Measurement

Question:

Can you measure how much metal expands when heated?

Hypothesis:

Yes, by "magnifying" a measurement of the change in length of a metal, you can estimate the true change.

Materials:

- **an adult**
- hollow metal tube(s) about a meter (yard) long of brass, steel, or copper from hardware store or science supply company
- board longer than tube(s)
- tape
- clothespin
- C-clamp
- protractor
- scissors
- light cardboard
- T-pin
- rubber band
- thumbtack
- rubber tubing
- source of steam such as a flask and hot plate
- tubing larger than a thermometer bulb
- thermometer, 20–100°C
- saucer
- meterstick or ruler
- thread
- roll of duct tape
- pencil
- long sheet of paper

Ask an adult to help with this experiment because you will be working with steam. To see just how much a solid expands when heated, you need to make careful measurements. As you saw in the previous experiment, a metal expands very little when heated. Therefore, you will have to magnify any change in length to accurately measure the amount the length changes.

Lengthwise (linear) expansion is measured as the change in length per unit length per degree. Suppose, for example, that a metal tube 1 m long expands 1.0 mm (0.001 m) when its temperature changes by 100°C. Its expansion would be expressed as:

$$0.001m \div 1m \div 100°C = 0.00001/°C$$

Figure 26.

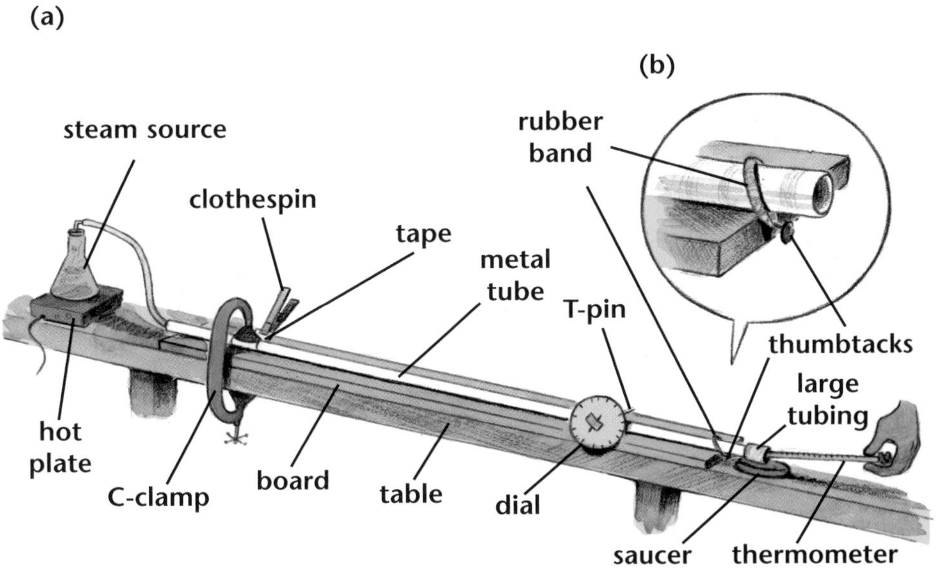

(a)

(b)

steam source

rubber band

clothespin

tape

metal tube

T-pin

thumbtacks

large tubing

hot plate

C-clamp

board

table

dial

saucer

thermometer

a) The drawing shows an experiment to measure the expansion of a metal tube.
b) A rubber band and thumbtack can hold the metal tube firmly on the T-pin.

Procedure:

1. Obtain one or more hollow metal tubes about one meter (1 yd) long. Place one of the tubes on a long board as shown in Figure 26a. Wrap a piece of tape around the tube close to one end.

2. Clamp a clothespin on the tape. Use a C-clamp to hold the clothespin in place so the tube can not move. Use a protractor, scissors, and a piece of light cardboard to make a circular dial that is divided into 10-degree intervals.

3. Push a T-pin through the center of the dial. Tape the T-part of the pin to the dial. Slide the pin under the free end of the tube. When the tube expands, the dial will turn. A rubber band and thumbtack (Figure 26b) over the end of the tube can be used to hold the tube firmly down against the pin without preventing the tube from expanding.

4. Use rubber tubing to connect the fixed end of the tube to a source of steam. A piece of tubing larger than a thermometer bulb should be attached to the end of the tube that is free to move. Put a saucer under the open end of the tube to collect condensed steam.

5. Measure and record the length of the tube between the point where it is securely fastened and the pin that will turn when the metal tube is heated by the steam. Record, too, the temperature of the room, which will be the same as the temperature of the metal tube at the beginning of the experiment. Set the dial so that the zero degree mark is in line with the edge of the board.

6. **Ask an adult** to heat the steam generator (perhaps a kettle of water on a stove) to force steam through the metal tube. After the tube stops expanding, record the angle through which the pin turned. Then place a thermometer bulb in the large piece of tubing at the free end of the metal tube and measure the temperature of the steam coming from the metal tube.

What temperature change did the metal tube undergo as it expanded?

7. To find the metal tube's change in the length, you will need the diameter of the pin that turned. This can be obtained by wrapping a piece of thread around the pin ten times. Then lay that length of thread on a ruler and divide its length by ten. This will give you the pin's circumference. How can you find its diameter? Remember: Diameter is equal to circumference divided by π (pi).

How can you use the angle through which the dial turned and the diameter of the pin to find the distance the pin rolled? As you can see from Figure 27, the expansion of the metal will be twice the distance that the pin traveled. This is because the pin rolls along the board; it does not turn in place.

8. To convince yourself of this, place a ruler on a roll of duct tape. Mark a point directly below one end of the ruler on a long sheet of paper. Make a second mark at the base of the roll of tape.

9. Slowly roll the duct tape through half a turn. You will see that the end of the ruler moves twice as far as the roll of tape.

Results and Conclusions

From your measurements, calculate the expansion for this metal per meter per degree. For example, suppose the length of the metal tube from clothespin to pin was 0.8 m and the temperature of the metal rose from 20°C to 100°C when the dial turned 60 degrees. If the pin's diameter was 1 mm, it rolled 60/360ths of its circumference, which is π times its diameter. Therefore, it turned a distance of:

$$\pi \times 1 \text{ mm} \times 60/360 = 0.52 \text{ mm}$$

Figure 27.

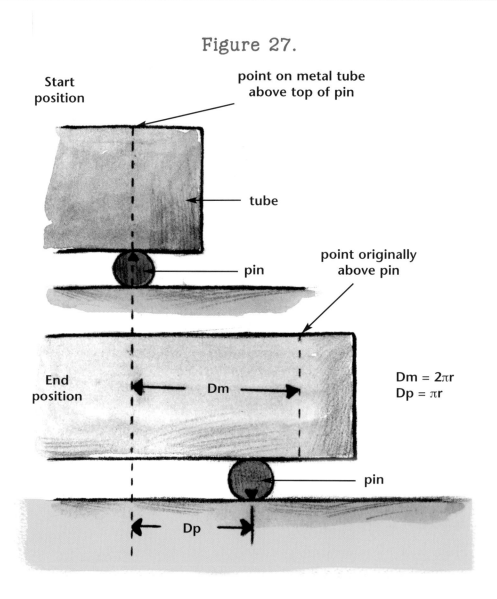

The diagram shows that the metal tube expands twice as far as the pin turns. If the pin makes half a turn, as shown, it moves a distance Dp, which is equal to half its circumference or π (pi) times its radius. Meanwhile, the tube will have expanded twice as far as the pin turned, a distance Dm, which is equal to π times the pin's diameter or 2π times its radius (r).

This means the metal actually expanded 1.04 mm, because 0.52 mm x 2 = 1.04 mm.

Now, to express the expansion as the change in length per unit length per degree, you have to divide the change in length by the length of the tube and by the tube's change in temperature. Consequently, the expansion of this particular metal in the example given would be:

$$1.04 \text{ mm} \div 800 \text{ mm} \div 80°C = 0.000016/°C$$

What is the expansion per length per degree of the tube you tested? The number you calculate is called the *linear coefficient of thermal expansion* for the metal you tested.

If possible, find the coefficients of some other solids. You might try tubes made of brass, steel, copper, and aluminum. Compare your results with those shown in Table 1.

Table 1:
Linear Coefficients of Thermal Expansion for Some Solids.

Solid	Linear Coefficient of Expansion (per °C)	Solid	Linear Coefficient of Expansion (per °C)
aluminum	0.000023	iron	0.000012
brass	0.000018	platinum	0.000009
copper	0.000017	silver	0.000019
glass (window)	0.000017	quartz	0.0000004
glass (Pyrex)	0.000003	gold	0.000014

EXPERIMENT 5.3

A Practical Use for the Expansion of Metals

Question:

How does a thermostat work?

Hypothesis:

Bimetallic strips that expand and contract with temperature changes are used in thermostat control switches.

Materials:

- **an adult**
- metal cutters
- tin can
- aluminum flashing
- epoxy glue
- board
- pencil or marking pen
- C-clamp
- heavy weight such as a brick or pile of books
- chair, stool, or table
- sheet of cardboard or heavy paper
- candle and/or matches

On a cold day you might turn up the thermostat in your home. A thermostat is really a switch that is turned on and off by changes in temperature. The switch opens and closes by means of a bimetallic strip, which consists of two strips of different metals that are fastened firmly together. As the strip warms or cools, it bends because the two metals expand or contract by different amounts over the same temperature change.

You can make a bimetallic strip similar to the ones found in thermostats.

Procedure:

1. **Ask an adult** to cut and straighten a 2.5-centimeter-wide (1-in-wide) strip of thin steel, about 15 to 30 centimeters (6 to 12 in) long, from an ordinary "tin" can. **Ask the adult** to cut a similar strip from a piece of aluminum flashing.

2. Spread epoxy glue along one side of each strip. Put the two strips together against the glue.

3. Hold them firmly together by putting them under a board with a heavy weight on it.

When the glue has dried, the two metals will be firmly stuck together.

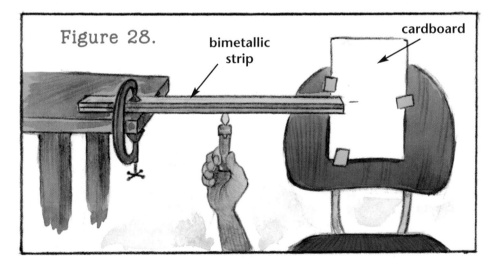

Notice how a bimetallic strip bends when heated.

4. Use a C-clamp to fasten one end of the bimetallic strip to the edge of a chair, stool, or table.

5. Fix a sheet of cardboard or heavy paper beside the other end of the strip as shown in Figure 28. Make a mark on the sheet to indicate the position of the free end of the strip.

6. Next, **ask the adult** to heat the bimetallic strip with a burning match or candle. Notice how the metal bends. Which metal expanded more, steel or aluminum?

Science Project Ideas

- Build other bimetallic strips using different metals. Which of the bimetallic strips you tested bent the most when heated? Which combination bent the least?

- From the data in Table 1, which two metals listed would make the most sensitive thermostat?

EXPERIMENT 5.4

Expansion and Contraction of Liquids

Question:

Do liquid properties change when they are heated and cooled?

Hypothesis:

Yes, almost all liquids expand when heated and contract when cooled.

Materials:

- clear drinking straw
- petroleum jelly
- one-hole rubber stopper or modeling clay or plasticine
- test tube
- water, hot and cold
- scissors
- light cardboard
- clear tape
- pencil or marking pen
- heavy drinking glass
- large (12 oz) Styrofoam cup
- rubbing alcohol

After measuring the expansion of solids, you would probably expect liquids to expand or contract very little. Consequently, it makes sense to magnify any expansion that occurs as you did with solids. You can do that by using a large volume of liquid that can expand only into a narrow tube. A test tube of liquid that can expand into a clear drinking straw will serve the purpose.

Procedure:

1. Coat one end of a drinking straw with a thin layer of petroleum jelly. Push this end of the straw through the hole in a one-hole rubber stopper that fits the test tube. If you do not have a rubber stopper, use modeling clay or plasticine to make a plug for the test tube.

2. Using scissors, cut a strip of light cardboard as long as the straw. Carefully tape the cardboard strip to the straw as shown.

3. Then fill the test tube to the brim with water. Insert the rubber stopper or plug into the mouth of the test tube and push it firmly into place. The water level should rise about halfway up the drinking straw as shown in Figure 29.

4. Let the test tube stand in a drinking glass for ten minutes so that the liquid reaches room temperature. Then, on the cardboard, mark the water level in the straw with a pencil or marking pen.

5. Place the test tube in a large Styrofoam cup filled with hot tap water. What happens to the water level in the straw? Mark its final level and measure the change in height with a ruler.

6. Remove the test tube from the hot water and place it in another Styrofoam cup filled with cold water. Observe and mark the final water level in the straw.

light cardboard

clear drinking straw

clear tape

water

one-hole rubber stopper or clay

Figure 29.

This apparatus can be used to measure the change in volume of water as it warms.

Results and Conclusions

Does water expand when heated? Does water contract when cooled?

Repeat the experiment using rubbing alcohol in the test tube in place of water. Be sure to refill the Styrofoam cup with "fresh" hot water. Does alcohol expand when heated? Does it contract when cooled? Do you have evidence that different liquids expand and contract by different amounts when heated?

From the results of your experiment, explain why the density of a liquid changes with temperature.

Science Project Ideas

- How could you increase the magnification of a liquid's expansion?

- Design and carry out experiments to find the *volume* coefficient of thermal expansion for water, rubbing alcohol, and glycerine.

EXPERIMENT 5.5

Expansion and Contraction of Gases

Question:

How do gases respond to heat and cold?

Hypothesis:

Gases expand when heated and contract when cooled.

Materials:

- test tube
- clear drinking straw
- one-hole rubber
  stopper, clay
  or plasticine
- petroleum jelly
- eyedropper
- water, hot and cold
- food coloring
- marking pen
- Styrofoam cup
- large, empty,
  narrow-necked,
  rigid plastic bottle
- drinking glass
- balloon
- refrigerator
- freezer
- cloth

Again, by carrying out experiments you can discover how gases respond to heat and cold. You can use the test tube, clear drinking straw, and one-hole rubber stopper or clay you used in the previous experiment.

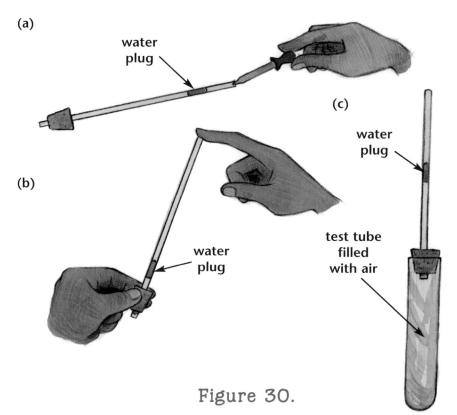

(a)

water
plug

(b)

(c)

water
plug

water
plug

test tube
filled
with air

Figure 30.

This apparatus can be used to see how the
volume of a gas changes when heated.

Procedure:

1. As before, coat one end of the drinking straw with petroleum jelly. Push this end of the straw through the hole in the rubber stopper or through the clay or plasticine plug.

2. Add food coloring to a cup of water. Hold the straw sideways and use an eyedropper to put a drop of colored water into one end. The drop should form a water "plug" that fills a small section of the straw as shown in Figure 30a.

3. Tilt the straw slightly upright to make the water plug slide down to a point slightly above the stopper or clay plug.

4. Seal the top of the straw by placing one finger firmly against the top of the straw (Figure 30b). Then hold the straw upright. Your finger prevents changes in air pressure and prevents the water plug from falling farther down the straw.

5. Keep your finger on the top of the straw as you insert the rubber stopper or clay plug into the mouth of the empty test tube.

6. When you release your finger, the water plug should rise to about the center of the straw and remain there, as shown in Figure 30c.

7. Use a marking pen to mark the straw at the level of the bottom of the water plug. (If the water plug slides down, it means there is an air leak in the straw around the rubber stopper that must be sealed.)

8. Place the test tube in a Styrofoam cup filled with hot tap water. Watch the level of the water plug as the hot water warms the air in the test tube. Does air expand when heated?

9. Next, place the test tube in a Styrofoam cup filled with cold water. Does air contract when cooled?

Results and Conclusions

Based on your observations here and in the previous experiments, does air expand more or less per degree change in temperature than liquids?

Predictions About the Expansion of Gases

Turn a large, empty, narrow-necked, rigid plastic or glass bottle upside down. Place the mouth of the bottle under some water in a drinking glass. Predict what you will see emerging from the bottle when you warm the rest of the bottle with your hands or with a cloth soaked in hot water. How can you explain what you observe? What do you predict will happen if you cool it with a cloth soaked in cold water?

Next, pull the neck of an empty balloon over the mouth of a large (1 L or larger) glass or rigid plastic bottle. Predict what will happen to the balloon when you put the bottle in a pan of hot water. Were you right?

Predict what will happen if you put the bottle and balloon in a refrigerator for an hour. Try it! Were you right?

Predict what will happen if you put the bottle and balloon into a freezer for an hour. Did you make the right prediction?

EXPERIMENT 5.6

Water to Ice:
Some Strange Behavior

Question:
How does water differ from other matter when it freezes?

Hypothesis:
When water turns to ice, it expands, becoming less dense.

Materials:

- ice cube
- drinking glass
- water
- food coloring
- transparent plastic
  drinking straw
- small jar such as a
  baby food jar
- clay
- marking pen
- freezer

The solids, liquids, and gases that you have examined in this chapter all contract when cooled and expand when heated. Most substances continue to contract as they change from liquid to solid while freezing. And contraction continues as the solid is cooled further. Consequently, in most cases, the density of matter increases as its temperature decreases.

Procedure:

1. To see that this behavior is not always the case, however, place an ice cube in a glass of water. Does the ice sink or float?

   What does this tell you about the density of ice as compared with the density of water? Based on what you have seen, predict what will happen to the volume of a certain amount of water as it changes to ice.

2. To check your prediction, color a glassful of water by adding a drop or two of food coloring to it. Place a transparent plastic drinking straw in the water and stir.

3. Then place your finger firmly on the top of the immersed straw as shown in Figure 31a. Keep your finger on the straw so that water will remain in the straw when you lift it out of the glass.

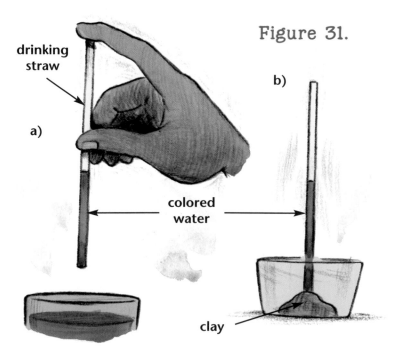

Figure 31.

drinking
straw

a)

b)

colored
water

clay

What happens to its volume when water freezes? How does this affect its density?

4. While keeping your finger on the top of the straw, carry the water to a small jar that contains a lump of clay. Press the bottom of the straw into the clay. When you remove your finger from the straw, the water should remain in place (Figure 31b).

5. When you are convinced that water is not leaking from the straw, mark the water level in the straw with a marking pen.

6. Place the jar that holds the clay and water-filled straw into a freezer. After about 30 minutes, open the freezer and look at the water level in the straw.

Results and Conclusions

Has the water turned to ice? What happened to the volume as the liquid water changed to solid ice? Did the experiment confirm your prediction?

 Science Project Ideas

- What significance does water's abnormal behavior have in nature? For example, what would happen if icebergs sank in the ocean and ice sank onto the bottoms of lakes and ponds?

- Design and carry out experiments to find the temperature at which water reaches its greatest density.

- Design and carry out experiments to find out what happens to the density of ice as its temperature falls farther and farther below its freezing point of 0°C (32°F).

EXPERIMENT 5.7

Expansion and Thermometers

Question:

How is expansion involved in making a thermometer?

Hypothesis:

Enclosed liquid in a thermometer visibly expands or contracts with temperature changes.

Materials:

- **an adult**
- 1-liter plastic soda bottle
- one-hole rubber stopper that fits the mouth of the bottle
- soap
- short piece of glass tubing or rigid plastic tubing
- 1-meter length of clear, flexible, plastic tubing
- measuring cup
- hot and cold water
- food coloring
- tape
- wall or post
- cold and warm damp cloths
- plastic soda straw
- eyedropper
- Styrofoam cups
- crushed ice or snow
- marking pen
- ruler
- household thermometer

Galileo probably made the world's first thermometer. He used the expansion of air as the basis for his thermometer. You can make a thermometer similar to Galileo's.

Procedure:

1. Find a 1-liter plastic soda bottle and a one-hole rubber stopper that fits the mouth of the bottle. **Ask an adult** to wet a short piece of glass tubing or rigid plastic tubing with some soap and insert it into the rubber stopper.

2. Add a 1-meter length of clear, flexible, plastic tubing to the short piece of tubing as shown in Figure 32a.

3. Color one cup of water with food coloring. Place the end of the clear tubing in the colored water. Tape the bottle to a wall or post.

4. Squeeze the bottle to force a few bubbles of air from it. When you release it, water should move about halfway up the tube and remain there.

5. To see that Galileo's thermometer can measure temperature, place a cold, damp cloth around the bottle. (Be careful not to squeeze the bottle!) What happens to the water level in the tubing?

6. Replace the cold cloth with a warm, damp one. What happens to the water level in the tubing?

Results and Conclusions

What is the main fault of this thermometer? **Hint:** *How will air pressure affect the water level in the tubing?* (Recall the barometer you built in Experiment 4.3.) You can build a smaller air thermometer using a plastic soda straw.

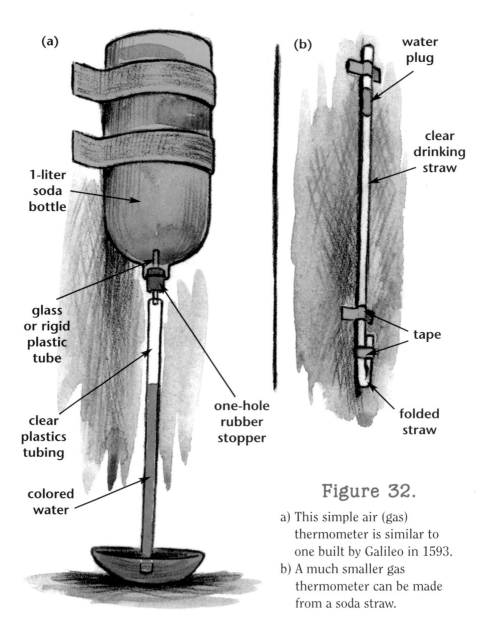

(a)

1-liter soda bottle

glass or rigid plastic tube

clear plastics tubing

colored water

one-hole rubber stopper

(b)

water plug

clear drinking straw

tape

folded straw

Figure 32.

a) This simple air (gas) thermometer is similar to one built by Galileo in 1593.
b) A much smaller gas thermometer can be made from a soda straw.

Procedure:

1. Hold the straw sideways. Use an eyedropper to inject a drop of colored water into one end of the straw.

2. Tilt the straw slightly upward to make the water plug slide about 5 cm (2 in) down the straw.

3. Keeping the water plug in place, flatten about 2 cm of the straw at its lower end and fold it over as shown in Figure 32b. Wrap the folded end of the straw firmly with the tape.

4. To make a scale for this thermometer, put the sealed end of the straw into a Styrofoam cup filled with crushed ice or snow. Observe how the water plug moves as the air contracts. Use a marking pen to mark the final level reached by the lower end of the water plug.

5. Fill a second Styrofoam cup with very hot tap water and insert the straw. Again, mark the final position reached by the lower end of the water plug after being in the hot water for a short time.

   You can assign your name to this temperature scale. You might call the temperature of the ice 0 degrees (0°). The temperature of the hot water might be called 10 degrees (10°).

6. Using a ruler, divide the distance between the 0° and 10° marks into ten equal lengths. You now have a temperature scale with a range of ten degrees. How could you extend your scale to read temperatures above and below the marks you have made?

Results and Conclusions

Use your gas thermometer to measure the temperature of the room you are in. What is the temperature of the room you are in according to your air thermometer? How does the temperature of the room on your scale compare with the temperature of the room according to a household thermometer?

Science Project Idea

- Modify the apparatus you used in Experiment 5.4 to make a liquid thermometer with a scale.

On the Matter of Matter

In this book you have seen that matter is anything that takes up space and has mass. It is made up of tiny particles, atoms and molecules, which exist in three different states—solid, liquid, and gas. The particles of matter are in constant motion and the speed at which they move governs the temperature of the matter.

You have seen, too, that we can identify different kinds of matter by their properties. Some are more dense than others; they differ in color, in boiling and melting temperatures, in the amount they expand or contract when heated or cooled, in how well they hold together, and in many other ways.

Appendix

SCIENCE SUPPLY COMPANIES

Carolina Biological Supply Company
2700 York Road
Burlington, NC 27215-3398
(800) 334-5551
http://www.carolina.com

Connecticut Valley Biological
   Supply Company
82 Valley Road
P.O. Box 326
Southampton, MA 01073
(800) 628-7748
http://www.ctvalleybio.com

Delta Education
80 Northwest Boulevard
P.O. Box 3000
Nashua, NH 03061-3000
(800) 258-1302
http://www.delta-education.com

Edmund Scientifics
60 Pearce Avenue
Tonawanda, NY 14150-6711
(800) 728-6999
http://scientificsonline.com

Educational Innovations, Inc.
362 Main Avenue
Norwalk, CT 06851
(888) 912-7474
http://www.teachersource.com

Fisher Science Education
4500 Turnberry Drive
Hanover Park, IL 60133
(800) 955-1177
http://www.fisheredu.com

Frey Scientific
80 Northwest Boulevard
Nashua, NH 03063
(800) 225-3739
http://www.freyscientific.com/

NASCO-Fort Atkinson
901 Janesville Avenue
P.O. Box 901
Fort Atkinson, WI 53538-0901
(800) 558-9595
http://www.nascofa.com/

NASCO-Modesto
4825 Stoddard Road
P.O. Box 3837
Modesto, CA 95352-3837
(800) 558-9595
http://www.nascofa.com

Sargent-Welch
P.O. Box 4130
Buffalo, NY 14217
(800) 727-4368
http://www.sargentwelch.com

Science Kit & Boreal Laboratories
777 East Park Drive
P.O. Box 5003
Tonawanda, NY 14151-5003
(800) 828-7777
http://sciencekit.com

Ward's Natural Science
P.O. Box 92912
Rochester, NY 14692-9012
(800) 962-2660
http://www.wardsci.com

Further Reading

Balwin, Carol. *States of Matter.* Chicago: Raintree, 2005.

Bochinski, Julianne Blair. *The Complete Workbook for Science Fair Projects.* Hoboken, N.J.: Wiley, 2005.

Claybourne, Anna. *The Nature of Matter.* Milwaukee, Wis.: Gareth Stevens Pub., 2007.

Haduch, Bill. *Science Fair Success Secrets: How to Win Prizes, Have Fun, and Think Like a Scientist.* New York: Dutton Children's Books, 2002.

Juettner, Bonnie. *Molecules.* Farmington Hills, Mich.: Kidhaven Press, 2005.

Stille, Darlene R. *Physical Change: Reshaping Matter.* Minneapolis, Minn.: Compass Point Books, 2006.

Vecchione, Glen. *Blue Ribbon Science Projects.* New York: Sterling Pub. Co., 2005.

Other Books by Robert Gardner

Gardner, Robert. *Ace Your Math and Measuring Science Project: Great Science Fair Ideas.* Berkeley Heights, N.J.: Enslow Publishers, Inc., 2010.

Gardner, Robert. *Physics Projects with a Light Box You Can Build.* Berkeley Heights, N.J.: Enslow Publishers, Inc., 2008.

Gardner, Robert, Madeline Goodstein, and Thomas R. Rybolt. *Ace Your Physical Science Project: Great Science Fair Ideas.* Berkeley Heights, N.J.: Enslow Publishers, Inc., 2010.

Internet Addresses

All Science Fair Projects
    <http://www.all-science-fair-projects.com/>

Exploratorium
    <http://www.exploratorium.edu/>

TryScience. "Experiments."
    < http://www.tryscience.org/experiments/experiments_home.html/>

Index